A WORLD OF CITIES

JAMES BROWN

CANDLEWICK STUDIO

an imprint of Candlewick Press

CONTENTS

The Great Fire of London started in a bakery on Pudding Lane on September 2, 1666.

London is the only city to have hosted the Summer Olympic Games three times.

The Roman Empire invaded Britain in 43 CE and went on to establish Londinium on the current site of the City of London. Londinium was abandoned in the fifth century.

The world's first traffic light was erected outside the Houses of Parliament in 1868.

It blew up the following year.

"When a man is tired of London, he is tired of life; for there is in London all that life can afford." — Samuel Johnson, 1777

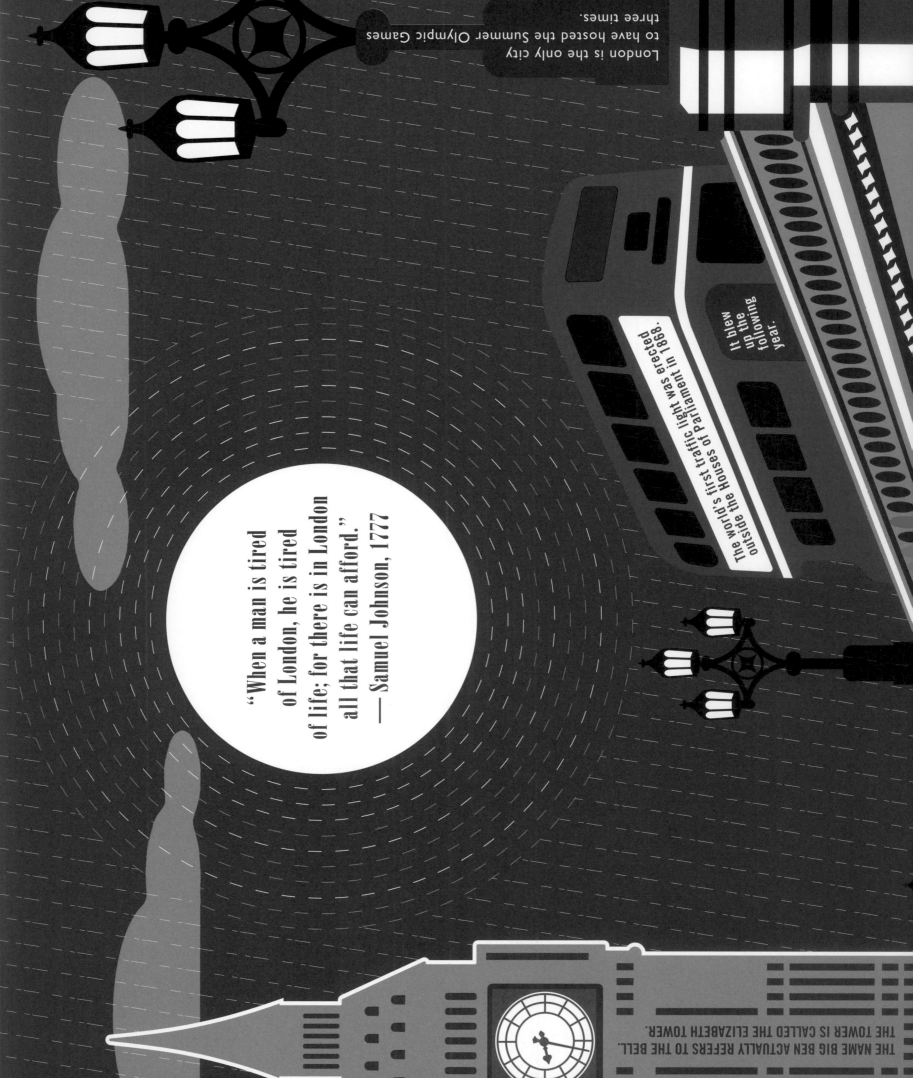

THE NAME BIG BEN ACTUALLY REFERS TO THE BELL. THE TOWER IS CALLED THE ELIZABETH TOWER.

Around 300 different languages are spoken in London — more than in any other city in the world.

Three of the top ten most visited museums and galleries in the world are in London, and it has a total of 857 art galleries.

The Tower of London was built as a royal palace about 900 years ago.

On one night during WWII, London was hit by an estimated 127,000 high explosives.

POPULATION: 8.8 MILLION

London has many subterranean rivers. The route of the largest, the Fleet, now exists as an underground sewer.

Each bridge in London has its own character and history. The most famous are London Bridge, Tower Bridge, and Westminster Bridge. The original medieval London Bridge lasted for more than 600 years and was often used to display the heads of traitors and criminals.

MUSEUMS: MORE THAN 200
BOOKSHOPS: 800
PUBLIC LIBRARIES: 380
TREES: 8 MILLION
SUBWAY STATIONS: 270
FESTIVALS: MORE THAN 250

The London Underground is the world's oldest subway system.

WITH THE EXCEPTIONS OF EDWARDS V AND VIII, WHO WERE NEVER CROWNED, EVERY ENGLISH MONARCH SINCE 1066 HAS BEEN CROWNED IN WESTMINSTER ABBEY.

LONDON

London is 47 percent green space. It has eight royal parks and more than a hundred commons, making it the world's largest urban forest.

Unusual street names in London include Ha-Ha Road in Woolwich, Quaggy Walk in Blackheath, and Cyclops Mews in Limehouse.

The Hong Kong area was first incorporated into imperial China in 214 BCE by the emperor Qin Shi Huang, famous for the Terracotta Army guarding his mausoleum.

Hong Kong territory is made up of Hong Kong Island, the Kowloon Peninsula, the New Territories, and more than 200 offshore islands.

The national symbol of Hong Kong is the orchid tree flower, known as the bauhinia.

In Hong Kong, more people live or work above the fourteenth floor than anywhere else, making it the world's most vertical city.

Standing at over 1,600 feet/500 meters, Victoria Peak is the highest point on Hong Kong Island.

Hong Kong has 316 buildings above 500 feet/150 meters and another three under construction — more than any other city.

After more than 150 years of British rule, China took back control of Hong Kong in July 1997.

HONG KONG

THE NAME HONG KONG MEANS "FRAGRANT HARBOR" IN THE ORIGINAL CANTONESE.

POPULATION: 7.4 MILLION

Cantonese and English are the official languages of Hong Kong.

The residents of Hong Kong have the world's longest life expectancy.

Hong Kong is one of the most densely populated cities on Earth. Since competition for living space is so fierce, new housing developments average less than 185 square feet/17 square meters and have been nicknamed "mosquito" apartments.

Hong Kong is famous for its junks, traditional wooden vessels that date back to the Han dynasty, in the second century. Junks usually have red sails because according to Chinese legend, the color red appeases the cloud dragon, who brings bad weather.

Hong Kong's harbor, Victoria Harbor, is world-famous for its skyline of skyscrapers. Every night, there's also a spectacular light and sound show, as lights and laser beams flash across the water in time to music.

Hong Kong is home to rare Chinese white dolphins — which are actually bubble-gum pink. It's estimated there are only around 60 left in Hong Kong's waters.

While Hong Kong has more skyscrapers than any other city in the world, about three-quarters of its territory is countryside.

NEW YORK

"The vertical city with unimaginable diamonds."
— Le Corbusier

New York City was founded in 1624 as a trading post by Dutch colonists and was then known as New Amsterdam.

THE EMPIRE STATE BUILDING, COMPLETED IN 1931, WAS THE WORLD'S TALLEST BUILDING FOR MORE THAN 40 YEARS.

NEW YORK HAS FIVE BOROUGHS:

STATEN ISLAND

MANHATTAN

BROOKLYN

QUEENS

THE BRONX

STANDING 305 FEET/93 METERS HIGH, THE STATUE OF LIBERTY IS A SYMBOL OF THE UNITED STATES AND ITS DEMOCRACY.

IN THE LATE NINETEENTH AND EARLY TWENTIETH CENTURIES, THE STATUE GREETED MILLIONS OF IMMIGRANTS AS THEY CAME TO THE AMERICAS BY SHIP.

ROUGHLY ONE IN EVERY 38 PEOPLE IN THE USA LIVES IN NEW YORK CITY.

VISITED BY 60 MILLION TOURISTS EVERY YEAR

"THE BIG APPLE"

NEW YORK HARBOR IS ONE OF THE WORLD'S LARGEST NATURAL HARBORS.

SECTIONS OF THE CITY'S GRANITE BEDROCK DATE TO MORE THAN 100 MILLION YEARS AGO.

THE MOST POPULOUS CITY IN THE UNITED STATES

MORE THAN 200 LANGUAGES ARE SPOKEN IN THE CITY.

POPULATION: 8.6 MILLION

TAXIS: 13,000

BROADWAY THEATERS: 40

GALLERIES: 1,000

MUSEUMS: 200

HIGH-RISE BUILDINGS: 6,000

SKYSCRAPERS: 50

Times Square was named after the *New York Times* moved its headquarters there in 1904.

Albert Einstein's eyeballs are stored in a safe-deposit box in New York City.

The Bosporus strait is a waterway that splits Istanbul into its European and Asian halves.

SINCE ITS FOUNDING, ISTANBUL HAS BEEN THE CAPITAL OF SOME OF THE MOST POWERFUL EMPIRES IN HISTORY: ROMAN, BYZANTINE, LATIN, AND OTTOMAN.

ISTANBUL

"If the Earth were a single state, Istanbul would be its capital."
—Napoleon Bonaparte

Istanbul is built on seven hills to match the seven hills of Rome. Their summits have been flattened through the ages, but their steep slopes are still visible.

ISTANBUL WAS FOUNDED AS BYZANTIUM AROUND 660 BCE. IT WAS THEN RENAMED CONSTANTINOPLE AFTER THE ROMAN EMPEROR CONSTANTINE IN 324 CE.

Built in the 1600s, the Sultan Ahmed Mosque is commonly known as the Blue Mosque after the blue tiles decorating its interior.

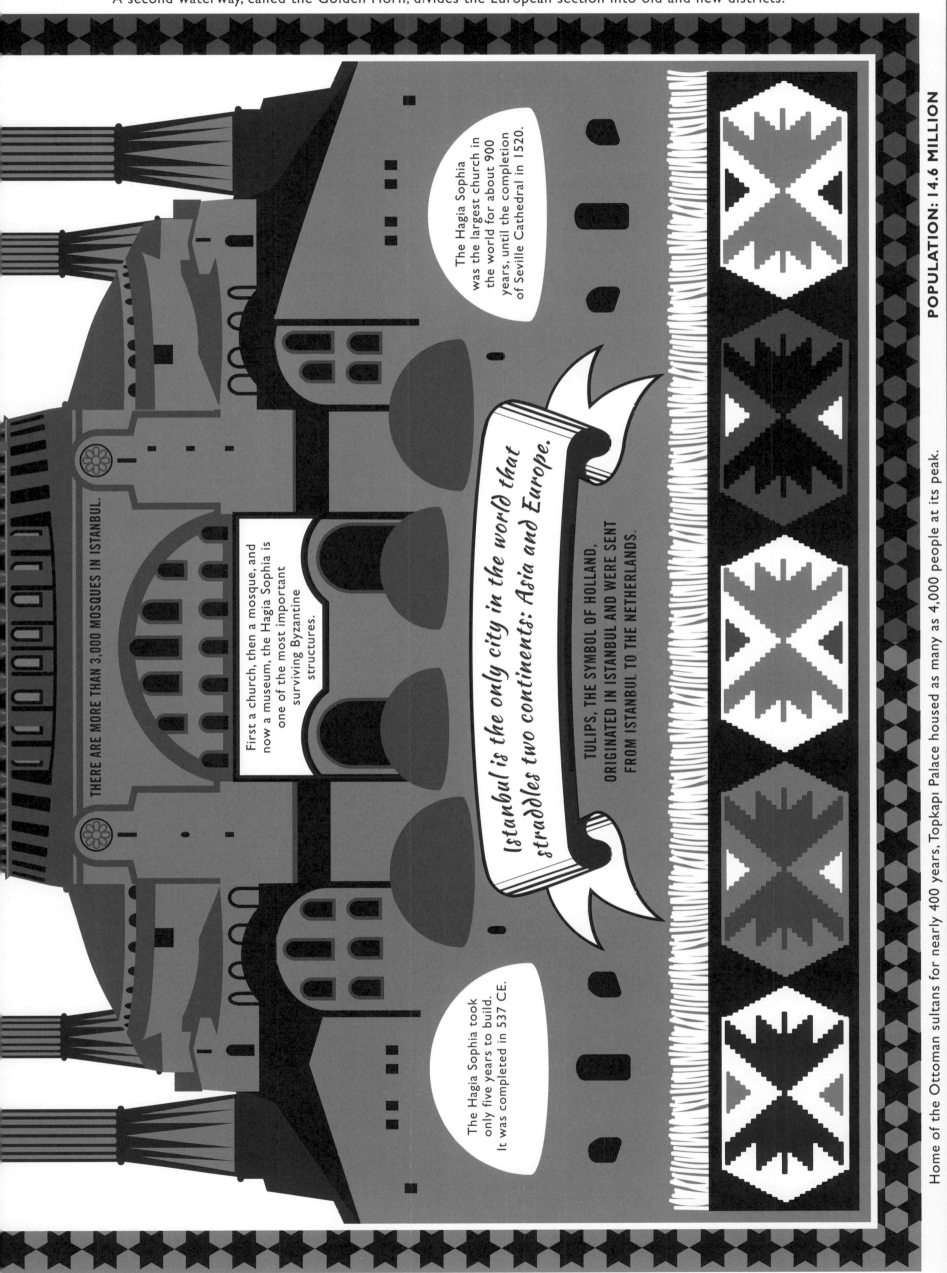

THERE ARE MORE THAN 3,000 MOSQUES IN ISTANBUL.

First a church, then a mosque, and now a museum, the Hagia Sophia is one of the most important surviving Byzantine structures.

The Hagia Sophia was the largest church in the world for about 900 years, until the completion of Seville Cathedral in 1520.

The Hagia Sophia took only five years to build. It was completed in 537 CE.

Istanbul is the only city in the world that straddles two continents: Asia and Europe.

TULIPS, THE SYMBOL OF HOLLAND, ORIGINATED IN ISTANBUL AND WERE SENT FROM ISTANBUL TO THE NETHERLANDS.

POPULATION: 14.6 MILLION

Home of the Ottoman sultans for nearly 400 years, Topkapı Palace housed as many as 4,000 people at its peak.

Istanbul's Grand Bazaar is one of the world's largest covered markets, with more than 3,000 shops spread over 61 streets.

Rio was founded in 1565 by the Portuguese. When Brazil achieved independence from Portugal in 1822, Rio became the capital and remained so until 1960.

"HERE THE MORNING IS BORN LIKE EVERYWHERE IN THE WORLD, BUT A FEELING VIBRATES THAT THINGS LOVED EACH OTHER DURING THE NIGHT." — CARLOS DRUMMOND DE ANDRADE

Rio de Janeiro

Rio's *Christ the Redeemer* statue, completed in 1931, stands 2,300 feet/700 meters above sea level on top of Corcovado Mountain.

The statue is made of concrete and covered in thousands of small stone tiles. All the materials had to be carried up Corcovado Mountain by railway.

Christ the Redeemer is often struck by lightning. In 2014, one of the statue's thumbs was badly damaged in a storm.

The statue is 125 feet/ 38 meters tall, including its pedestal, with arms that stretch 92 feet/ 28 meters.

The stars on Brazil's flag show the night sky as seen from Rio on November 15, 1889, the date Brazil overthrew its emperor and became a republic.

On New Year's Eve, people flock to the beach for a party. There are firework displays, and revelers push flower-filled boats out to sea in recognition of Yemanjá, the goddess of the sea.

POPULATION: 6.5 MILLION

RIO IS FAMOUS FOR ITS BEACHES, INCLUDING THE 2½-MILE-/4-KILOMETER-LONG COPACABANA BEACH.

Rio's harbor is studded by several mountains, including Sugarloaf Mountain, which rises 1,300 feet/396 meters above the waterfront. Glass-walled cable cars run from a ground station to the summit.

Legend has it that Portuguese explorers who landed in Rio in January 1502 thought the bay was the mouth of a river and named the area Rio de Janeiro ("River of January"), even though no river existed.

Every year, Rio de Janeiro hosts the biggest carnival in the world: more than 2 million people line the streets to enjoy floats, samba dancing, music, costumes, and marching bands.

Samba, a form of Brazilian music and dance, is hugely popular in Rio. There are more than 100 samba schools.

13

Rome has a walled city within it, the Vatican state, which is ruled by the bishop of Rome: the pope.

Rome sits on the shores of the Tiber River in central Italy. It was famously built on seven hills — the Aventine, Caelian, Capitoline, Esquiline, Palatine, Quirinal, and Viminal.

Rome has been the official capital of Italy since 1871.

and once known as the caput mundi — "capital of the world."

Rome was the capital of the Roman Empire

ROME

The Eternal City

Rome first grew into a powerful city as the seat of the Roman Republic, which lasted from 509 BCE to 27 BCE.

The Republic eventually controlled the whole of the Mediterranean region, making Rome a city of great importance.

Finished in 80 CE under the emperor Vespasian, the Colosseum is the world's largest amphitheater.

In imperial times, crowds flocked there to see gladiatorial fights, naval battles, animal hunts, and plays from classical mythology.

The Colosseum is made from stone columns and arches and can hold 80,000 spectators.

The emperor had a private entrance and watched the spectacles from the imperial box.

Built by tens of thousands of slaves, — there were 36 trapdoors, which were

Before each event, performers would wait in the rooms and passages hidden beneath the arena

The floor of the arena was covered in sand, sometimes dyed red to hide blood from the fights and hunts.

According to Catholic tradition, Saint Peter's Basilica is the burial place of Saint Peter. It's one of the holiest churches in Christendom.

POPULATION: 2.9 MILLION

LEAD TO ROME

ALL ROADS

Traffic police in Rome are known as the pizzardone.

The Pantheon, once a Roman temple, now a church, is one of the best-preserved ancient Roman buildings. Completed around 126 CE, it still has the world's largest unreinforced concrete dome.

According to legend, the founder of Rome, Romulus, and his twin brother, Remus, were abandoned on the banks of the Tiber and nursed by a she-wolf.

Beneath the city lie ancient catacombs: mazes of underground tunnels used as burial places.

15

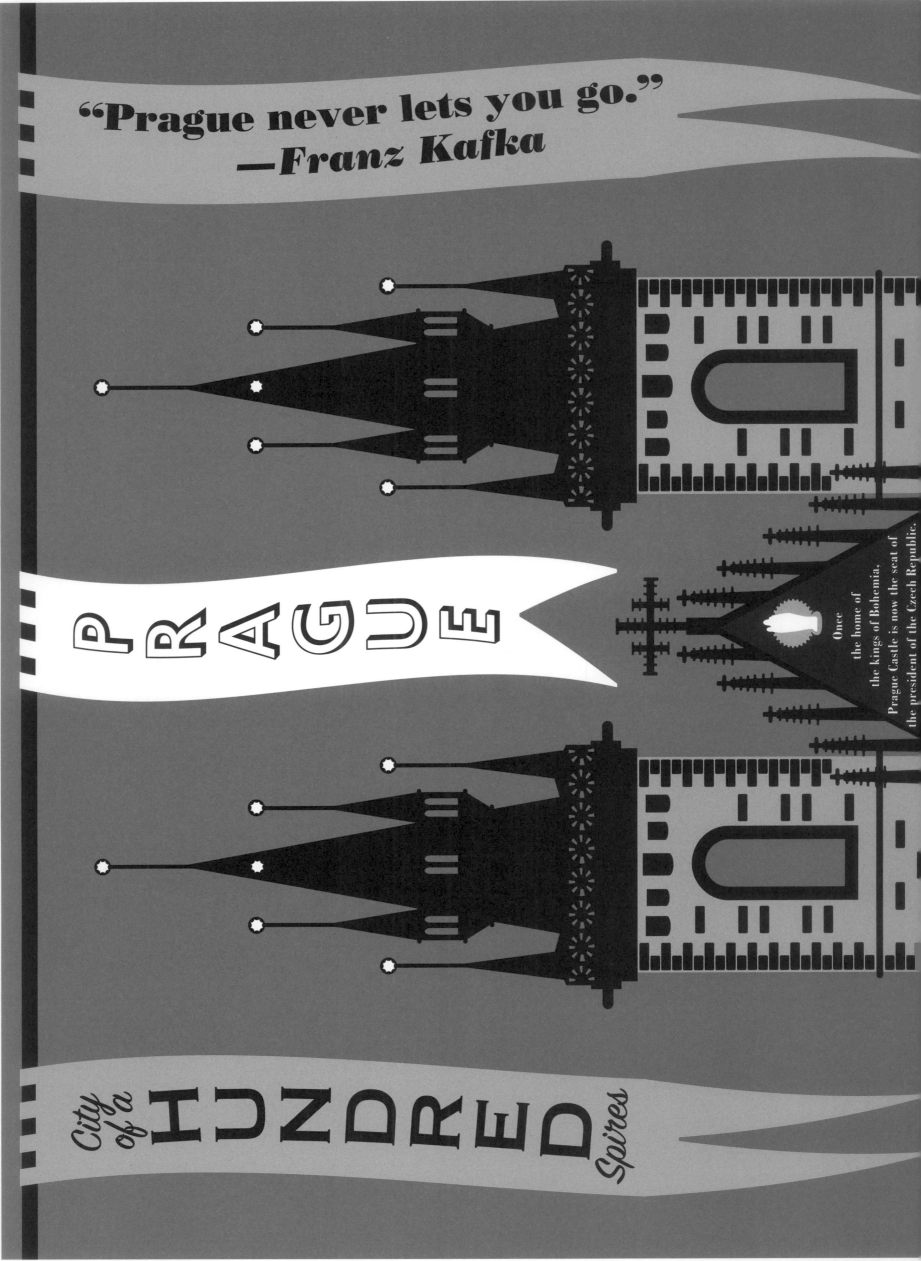

"Prague never lets you go."
—Franz Kafka

In early modern times, the Czech state and its surrounding districts were called the Lands of the Bohemian Crown and were ruled by Czech monarchs known as the kings of Bohemia.

PRAGUE

Once
the home of
the kings of Bohemia,
Prague Castle is now the seat of
the president of the Czech Republic.

City of a HUNDRED Spires

A hill, Petřín, 1,073 feet/327 meters high, rises from the center of Prague. An observation tower, a miniature Eiffel Tower, sits on the top.

Through its breeding program, Prague Zoo saved the last surviving subspecies of wild horse: more than 200 foals have been bred since 1959.

IN THE THIRTEENTH CENTURY, JEWS WERE EXPELLED FROM COUNTRIES ALL OVER EUROPE, AND MANY CAME TO PRAGUE, WHERE THEY WERE CONFINED TO THE JEWISH QUARTER. IT HAS THE OLDEST PRACTICING SYNAGOGUE IN EUROPE AND ONE OF THE EARLIEST SURVIVING JEWISH CEMETERIES.

The Velvet Revolution, the nonviolent overturn of power in 1989, began in Prague.

PRAGUE IS THE CAPITAL AND LARGEST CITY OF THE CZECH REPUBLIC. THE BEGINNINGS OF PRAGUE DATE FROM THE SECOND HALF OF THE NINTH CENTURY, WITH THE BUILDING OF PRAGUE CASTLE AND THE APPEARANCE OF THE FIRST INDEPENDENT SETTLEMENTS.

PRAGUE CASTLE IS THE CITY'S MOST POPULAR ATTRACTION AND THE LARGEST ANCIENT CASTLE IN THE WORLD.

ITS COURTYARDS AND BUILDINGS COVER AN AREA BIGGER THAN SEVEN FOOTBALL FIELDS.

The Old Town Square has the oldest still-working astronomical clock.

Its dial shows the position of the sun and moon in the sky.

The bridge has sixteen arches and 30 statues of saints along its sides.

The bridge connects Prague Castle to the city's Old Town.

Built in 1357, the Charles Bridge, which crosses the Vltava, is the oldest in Prague.

The Vltava River, the longest in the Czech Republic, flows right through the heart of Prague.

The composer Leoš Janáček studied at the Prague Organ School. He was so poor, he had to make do with a keyboard drawn on his tabletop.

Beer is served almost everywhere in Prague, even in breakfast cafés.

POPULATION: 1.3 MILLION

Many Hollywood films have been shot in Prague, including Casino Royale, Mission: Impossible, and Amadeus.

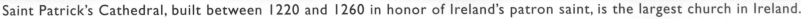
Saint Patrick's Cathedral, built between 1220 and 1260 in honor of Ireland's patron saint, is the largest church in Ireland.

Known as the Fair City, Dublin was founded in 988 CE, having first been settled by Christians and then by Vikings. The river Liffey divides the city into the Northside and the Southside.

It is now one of the most photographed sites in Dublin. It's so called because you once had to pay half a penny to cross it.

The Ha'penny Bridge, built in 1816, is an old iron footbridge over the river Liffey.

"When I die, Dublin will be written in my heart." —James Joyce

Dublin is known for its Georgian architecture, seen in buildings such as the Four Courts and the Custom House, with their grand archways, pillars, and domes.

The street signs in Dublin are written in both Gaelic and English, although most people in Dublin speak English.

DUBLIN

Dublin's University, Trinity College, was founded by Queen Elizabeth I of England in 1592.

June 16 is Bloomsday, when fans of James Joyce take to the city in costume, reading from his novel *Ulysses* and following the journey of the main character, Leopold Bloom, across the city.

Trinity College houses the Book of Kells, an illuminated manuscript made by Irish monks in around 800 CE, containing the four Gospels in Latin. Highly illustrated, its leaves are made of vellum. Its pigments include blue made from indigo or woad, orpiment (yellow arsenic sulfide) to make a vibrant yellow, and red lead.

POPULATION: 1.2 MILLION

Dublin has the youngest population in Europe, with around 40 percent under the age of 30.

Dublin Castle, which became the center of Norman power in Ireland, was founded in 1204.

Over the centuries, Dublin Castle has entertained many famous visitors, including Queen Victoria, Charles Dickens, Princess Grace of Monaco, John F. Kennedy, Nelson Mandela, and Queen Elizabeth II.

Dublin has produced many world-famous authors, including:

William Butler Yeats
George Bernard Shaw
James Joyce
Samuel Beckett
Oscar Wilde
Jonathan Swift
Bram Stoker

It has a typical Norman design, with a central square bounded by tall walls and a round defensive tower in each of the four corners.

The remains of Saint Valentine lie in Dublin's Whitefriar Street Church.

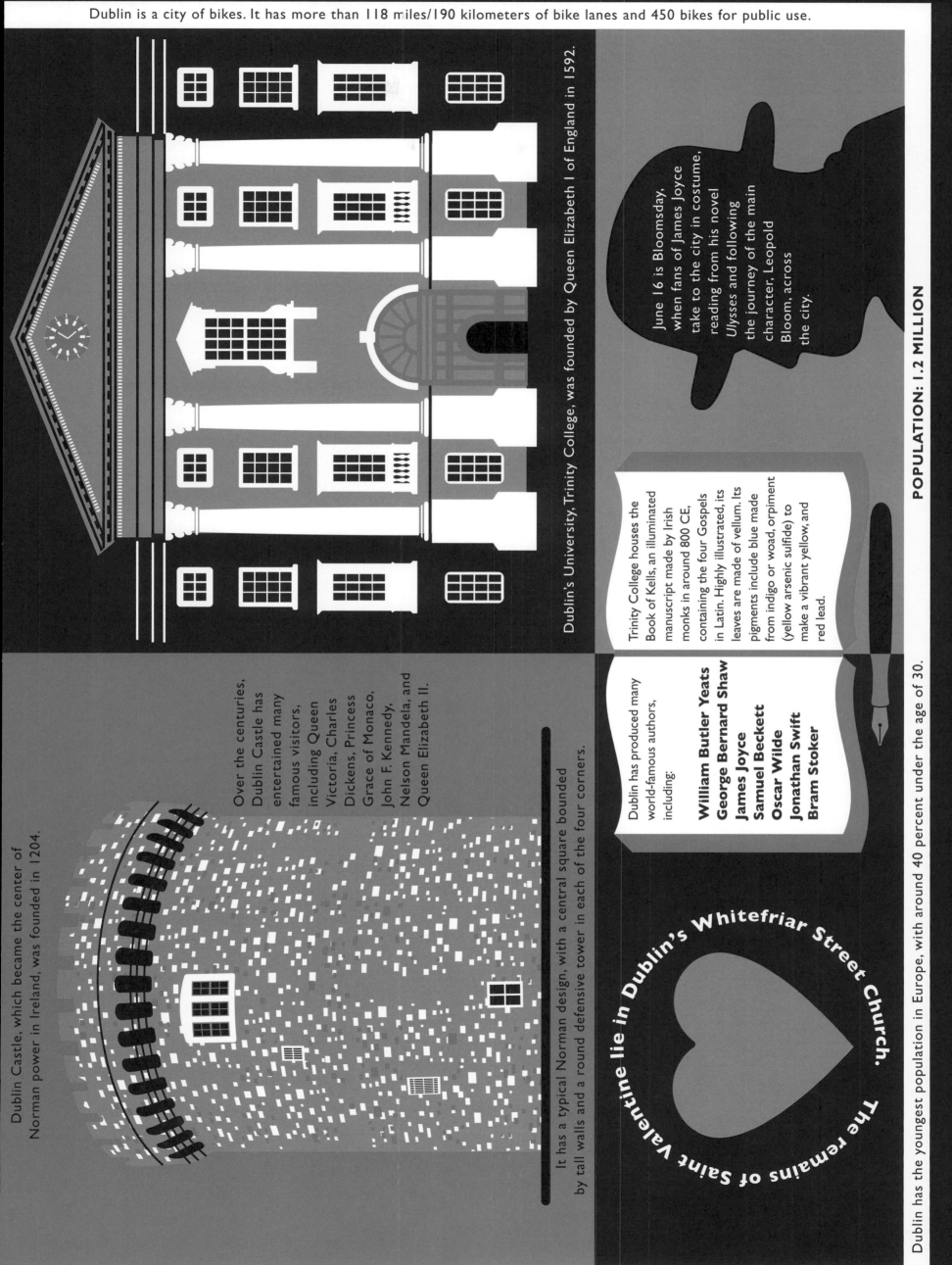

Seoul is South Korea's capital and largest city: the present-day site of the city, near the Han River, was first settled around 4000 BCE.

SEOUL

SEOUL IS SURROUNDED BY MOUNTAINS, THE HIGHEST OF WHICH IS BUKHANSAN, OR BUKHAN MOUNTAIN, AT 2,744 FEET/836.5 METERS.

SEOUL IS KNOWN FOR ITS HIGH POPULATION DENSITY, WHICH IS ALMOST TWICE THAT OF NEW YORK AND EIGHT TIMES GREATER THAN THAT OF ROME.

SEOUL'S GWANGJANG MARKET IS ONE OF THE OLDEST AND LARGEST TRADITIONAL MARKETS IN SOUTH KOREA. VENDORS SELL FOOD, CLOTHING, AND MEDICINES.

TRADITIONAL FOOD IN SEOUL INCLUDES THE HANJEONGSIK—A MULTICOURSE BANQUET—AND HOTTEOK, WHICH ARE HOT, CRISPY PANCAKES.

Rising 777 feet/236.7 meters from the top of Namsan Mountain in central Seoul, the Namsan Seoul Tower is the second-highest point in the city. Built as a communications tower, it now has a revolving restaurant at the top and an observatory with high-powered telescopes for gazing over the city.

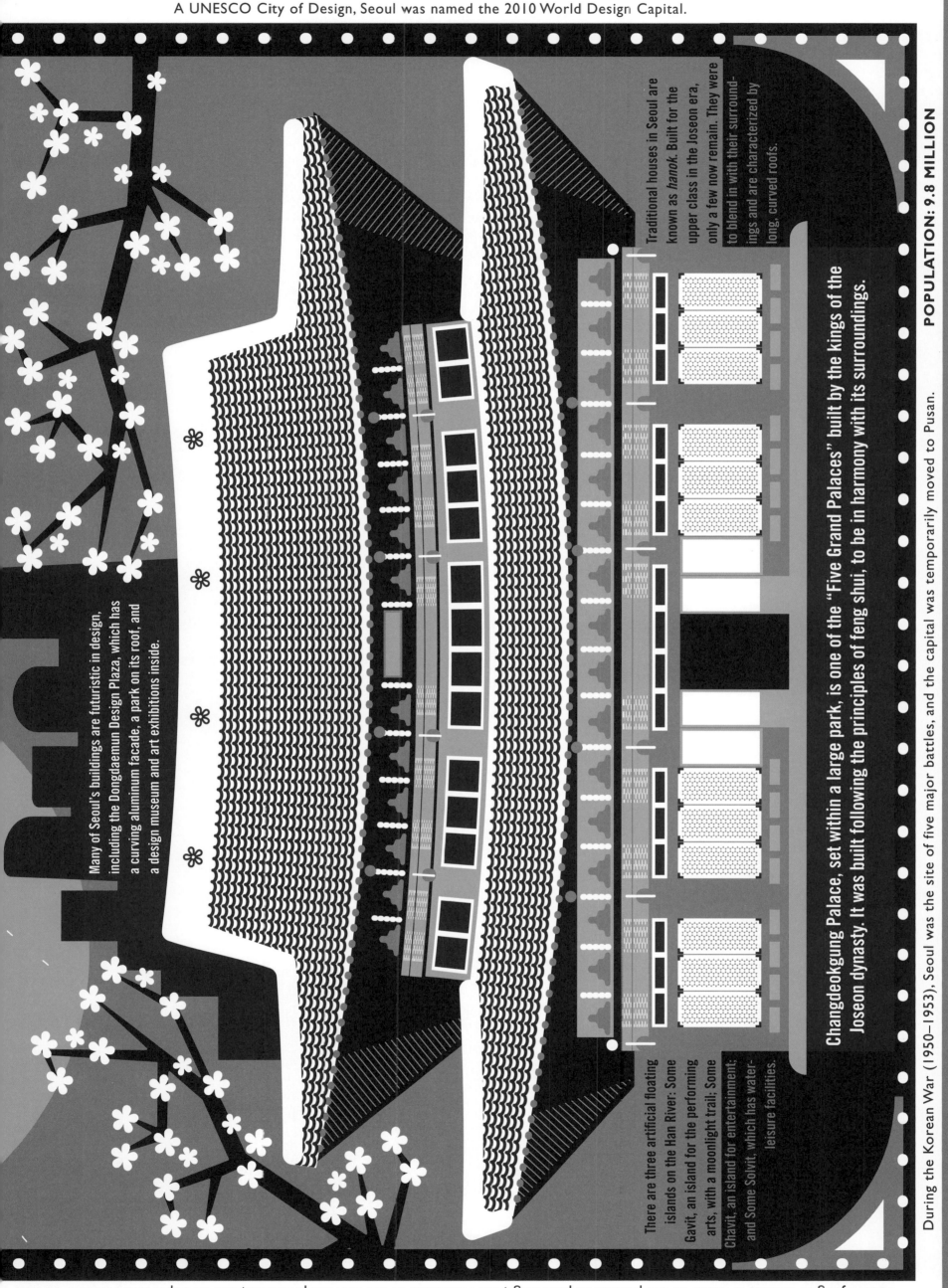

Many of Seoul's buildings are futuristic in design, including the Dongdaemun Design Plaza, which has a curving aluminum facade, a park on its roof, and a design museum and art exhibitions inside.

There are three artificial floating islands on the Han River: Some Gavit, an island for the performing arts, with a moonlight trail; Some Chavit, an island for entertainment; and Some Solvit, which has water-leisure facilities.

Traditional houses in Seoul are known as *hanok*. Built for the upper class in the Joseon era, only a few now remain. They were to blend in with their surroundings and are characterized by long, curved roofs.

Changdeokgung Palace, set within a large park, is one of the "Five Grand Palaces" built by the kings of the Joseon dynasty. It was built following the principles of feng shui, to be in harmony with its surroundings.

POPULATION: 9.8 MILLION

During the Korean War (1950–1953), Seoul was the site of five major battles, and the capital was temporarily moved to Pusan.

Seoul's Jongno district is home to the palaces of past kings, the residence of the current president, and an important business center.

21

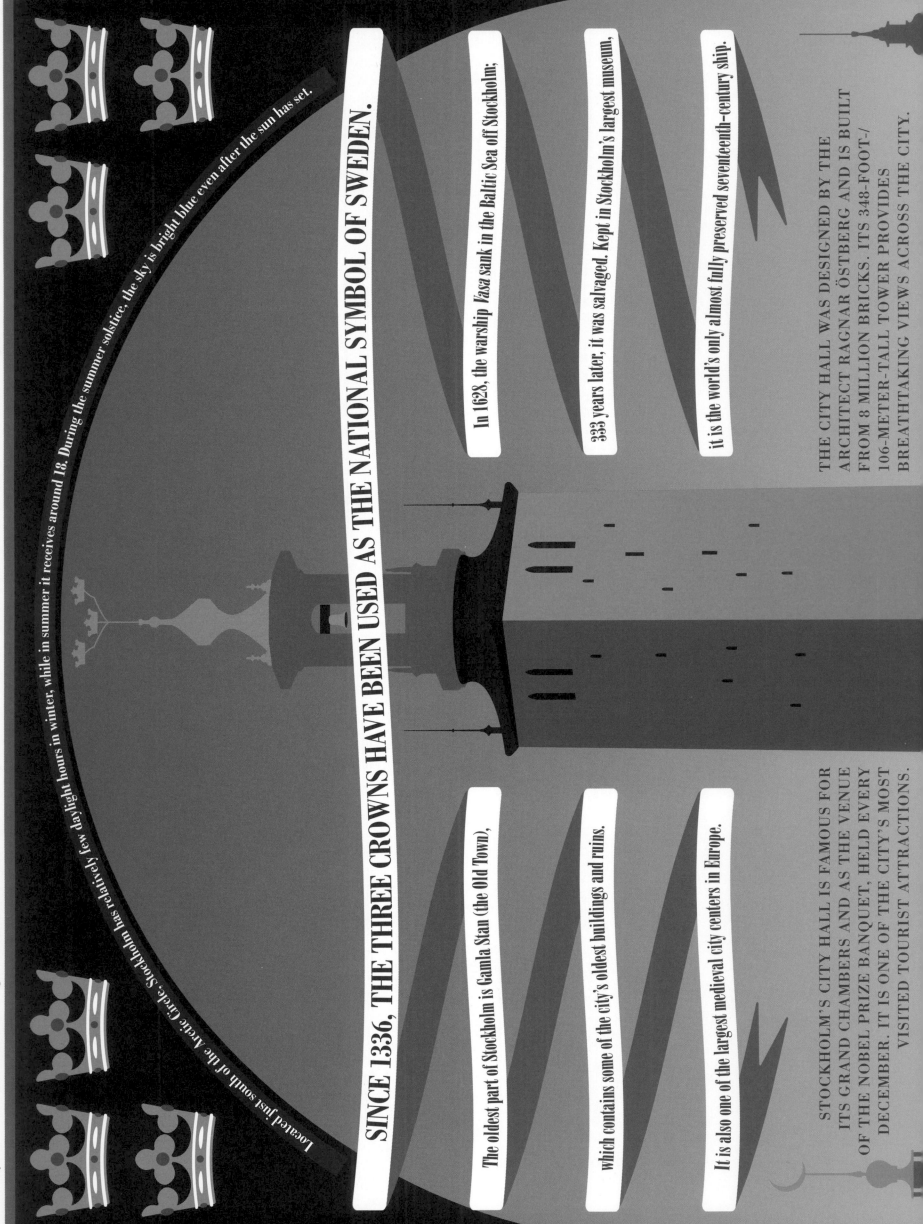

The official residence of the king and queen of Sweden, the baroque Royal Palace has more than 600 rooms spread across seven floors.

As the capital of the Lake Mälaren region, Stockholm can trace its origins back to two far older cities: Birka (around 750 CE) and Sigtuna (around 1000 CE), both founded by the Vikings.

Located just south of the Arctic Circle, Stockholm has relatively few daylight hours in winter, while in summer it receives around 18. During the summer solstice, the sky is bright blue even after the sun has set.

SINCE 1336, THE THREE CROWNS HAVE BEEN USED AS THE NATIONAL SYMBOL OF SWEDEN.

In 1628, the warship *Vasa* sank in the Baltic Sea off Stockholm;

333 years later, it was salvaged. Kept in Stockholm's largest museum,

it is the world's only almost fully preserved seventeenth-century ship.

THE CITY HALL WAS DESIGNED BY THE ARCHITECT RAGNAR ÖSTBERG AND IS BUILT FROM 8 MILLION BRICKS. ITS 348-FOOT-/106-METER-TALL TOWER PROVIDES BREATHTAKING VIEWS ACROSS THE CITY.

The oldest part of Stockholm is Gamla Stan (the Old Town),

which contains some of the city's oldest buildings and ruins.

It is also one of the largest medieval city centers in Europe.

STOCKHOLM'S CITY HALL IS FAMOUS FOR ITS GRAND CHAMBERS AND AS THE VENUE OF THE NOBEL PRIZE BANQUET, HELD EVERY DECEMBER. IT IS ONE OF THE CITY'S MOST VISITED TOURIST ATTRACTIONS.

The name Stockholm comes from *stock*, meaning "log," and *holm*, meaning "islet," although no one knows how the city came by its name.

The Royal Palace was built to replace the original Tre Kronor Palace, which was destroyed by a violent fire in 1697.

Stockholm hosts the annual Nobel Prize ceremonies and banquet at the Stockholm Concert Hall and City Hall, respectively. Founded by Swedish-born inventor Alfred Nobel and first awarded in 1901, the Nobel Prize recognizes outstanding contributions to physics, chemistry, medicine, and literature.

STOCKHOLM

OVER 30 PERCENT OF THE CITY IS MADE UP OF WATERWAYS, AND ANOTHER 30 PERCENT IS MADE UP OF PARKS AND GREEN SPACES.

POPULATION: 910,000

Past winners of Nobel Prizes include Marie Curie for chemistry, Albert Einstein for physics, and Bob Dylan for literature.

The narrowest alley in Gamla Stan is Mårten Trotzigs Gränd, only 35 inches/90 centimeters wide at its narrowest point.

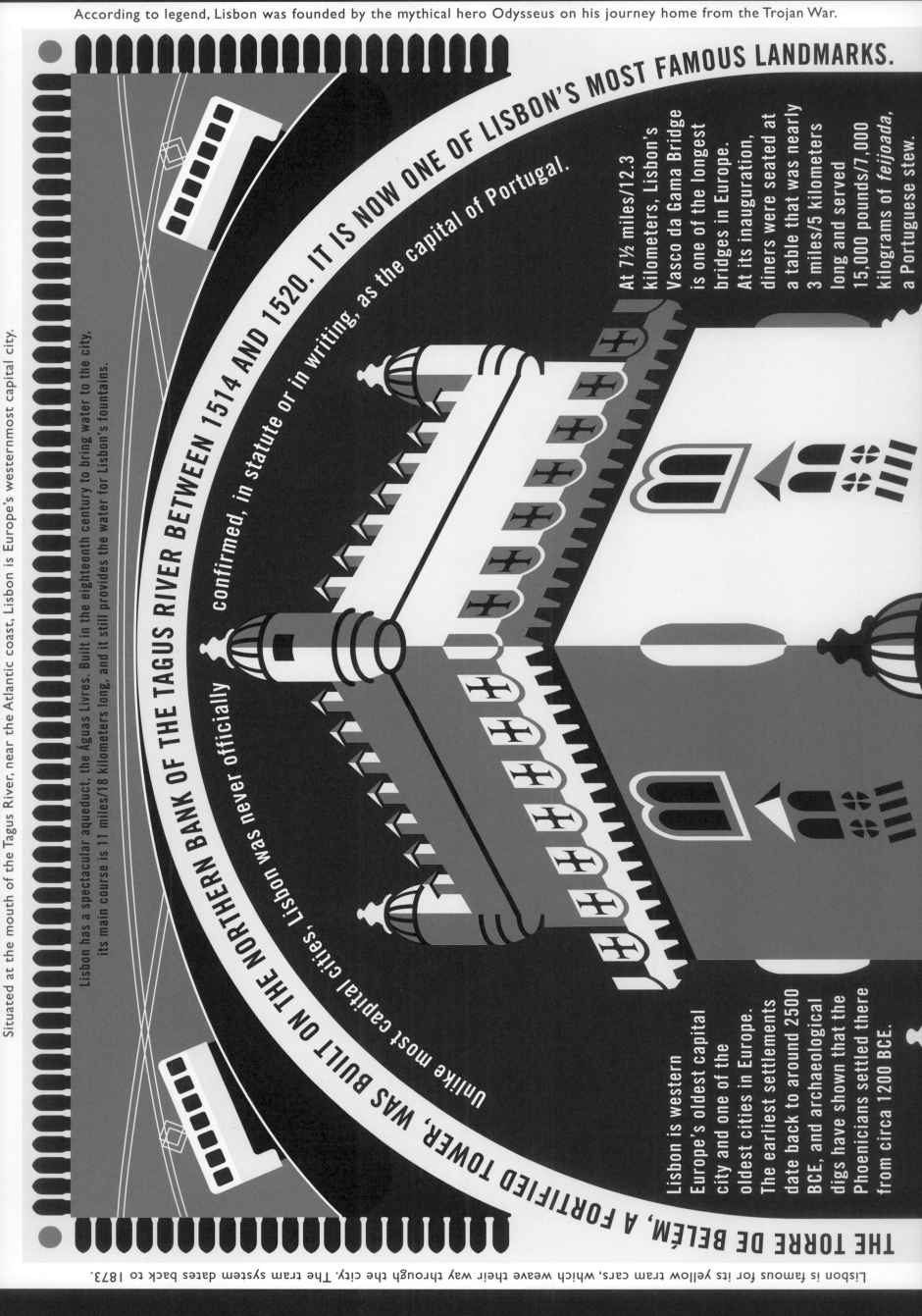

THE TORRE DE BELÉM, A FORTIFIED TOWER, WAS BUILT ON THE NORTHERN BANK OF THE TAGUS RIVER BETWEEN 1514 AND 1520. IT IS NOW ONE OF LISBON'S MOST FAMOUS LANDMARKS.

Unlike most capital cities, Lisbon was never officially confirmed, in statute or in writing, as the capital of Portugal.

Situated at the mouth of the Tagus River, near the Atlantic coast, Lisbon is Europe's westernmost capital city.

Lisbon has a spectacular aqueduct, the Águas Livres. Built in the eighteenth century to bring water to the city, its main course is 11 miles/18 kilometers long, and it still provides the water for Lisbon's fountains.

At 7½ miles/12.3 kilometers, Lisbon's Vasco da Gama Bridge is one of the longest bridges in Europe. At its inauguration, diners were seated at a table that was nearly 3 miles/5 kilometers long and served 15,000 pounds/7,000 kilograms of *feijoada*, a Portuguese stew.

Lisbon is western Europe's oldest capital city and one of the oldest cities in Europe. The earliest settlements date back to around 2500 BCE, and archaeological digs have shown that the Phoenicians settled there from circa 1200 BCE.

LISBON

POPULATION: 545,000

Five minutes' drive from the Torre de Belém, shown here, the ornate Gothic-style Jerónimos Monastery was begun in 1501 and took a hundred years to complete. It is one of Lisbon's main tourist attractions. For four centuries, the monastery was home to monks of the Order of Saint Jerome, whose spiritual role was, at least in part, to pray for the king's soul and the safe return of sailors.

First created by the monks of the Jerónimos Monastery, little custard tartlets called *pastéis de nata* are now a Portuguese specialty.

"OH SALTED SEA, HOW MUCH OF YOUR SALT IS PORTUGUESE TEARS?"
—FERNANDO PESSOA

Lisbon has a secret attraction—the Galerias Romanas—which is open for only a few days each year. It is an underground labyrinth of vaults dating from around the first century CE, built by the Romans, possibly for storage or as a water supply.

Lisbon is home to a legendary flea market, the Feira da Ladra, whose name means "Market of Thieves."

On November 1, 1755, Lisbon was hit by a fearsome earthquake that destroyed about 85 percent of the city.

SAN FRANCISCO

The city was founded in 1776, when Spanish colonists established the Presidio of San Francisco settlement on the peninsula and the Mission San Francisco de Asís a few miles away.

The first Europeans to reach the site of San Francisco were a group of Spanish explorers who came overland from Mexico in 1769. Before then, western explorers traveling by boat had always missed the bay because of the area's thick fog.

"SAN FRANCISCO HAS ONLY ONE DRAWBACK— 'TIS HARD TO LEAVE." —RUDYARD KIPLING

The city has more than 50 hills. Some neighborhoods are named after the hill on which they're situated, including Nob Hill and Russian Hill. The eight sharp turns and distinctive red paving of Lombard Street were designed in 1922 to help cars drive safely down the steep slope.

In 1906, a massive earthquake struck San Francisco. More than 3,000 people died and three-quarters of the city was destroyed.

Golden Gate Bridge is 1.7 miles/2.7 kilometers long, stretching from San Francisco to the Marin Headlands.

Alcatraz Island, 1½ miles/2.5 kilometers from the shore, was used as a federal prison from 1934 to 1963. It once housed famous convicts such as Al Capone but is now a major tourist attraction.

IN 1846, THE UNITED STATES TOOK SAN FRANCISCO FROM MEXICO. THEN IN 1848 CAME THE GOLD RUSH, AND WITH IT A MASSIVE BOOM IN THE CITY'S POPULATION AS PROSPECTORS FLOODED IN.

The bridge's two main cables use 80,000 miles/125,000 kilometers of wire. Looped around the equator in a single strand, they would circle the planet three times.

The largest and best-known city park is Golden Gate Park, which stretches from the center of the city to the Pacific Ocean in the west. It is home to the Conservatory of Flowers, a Japanese tea garden, and the San Francisco Botanical Garden.

POPULATION: 865,000

27

Both the bendy straw and the modern-day fortune cookie were invented in San Francisco.

San Francisco has several nicknames, including "the City by the Bay," "Fog City," "San Fran," and "Frisco."

Perched on top of the steep hill of Montmartre, Basilique du Sacré-Cœur is the highest point in Paris at 426 feet/130 meters above sea level.

ONE OF THE MOST VISITED CITIES IN THE WORLD!

THE CITY OF LIGHT

PARIS

THE CAPITAL OF FRANCE

FLUCTUAT NEC MERGITUR (TOSSED BUT NOT SUNK)

THE EIFFEL TOWER

PARIS HAS MORE THAN 400 PARKS AND GARDENS . . .

MORE THAN 9,000 RESTAURANTS . . .

PARIS'S OLDEST CAFÉ, CAFÉ PROCOPE, OPENED IN 1686.

THERE ARE 26 COUTURE HOUSES IN PARIS.

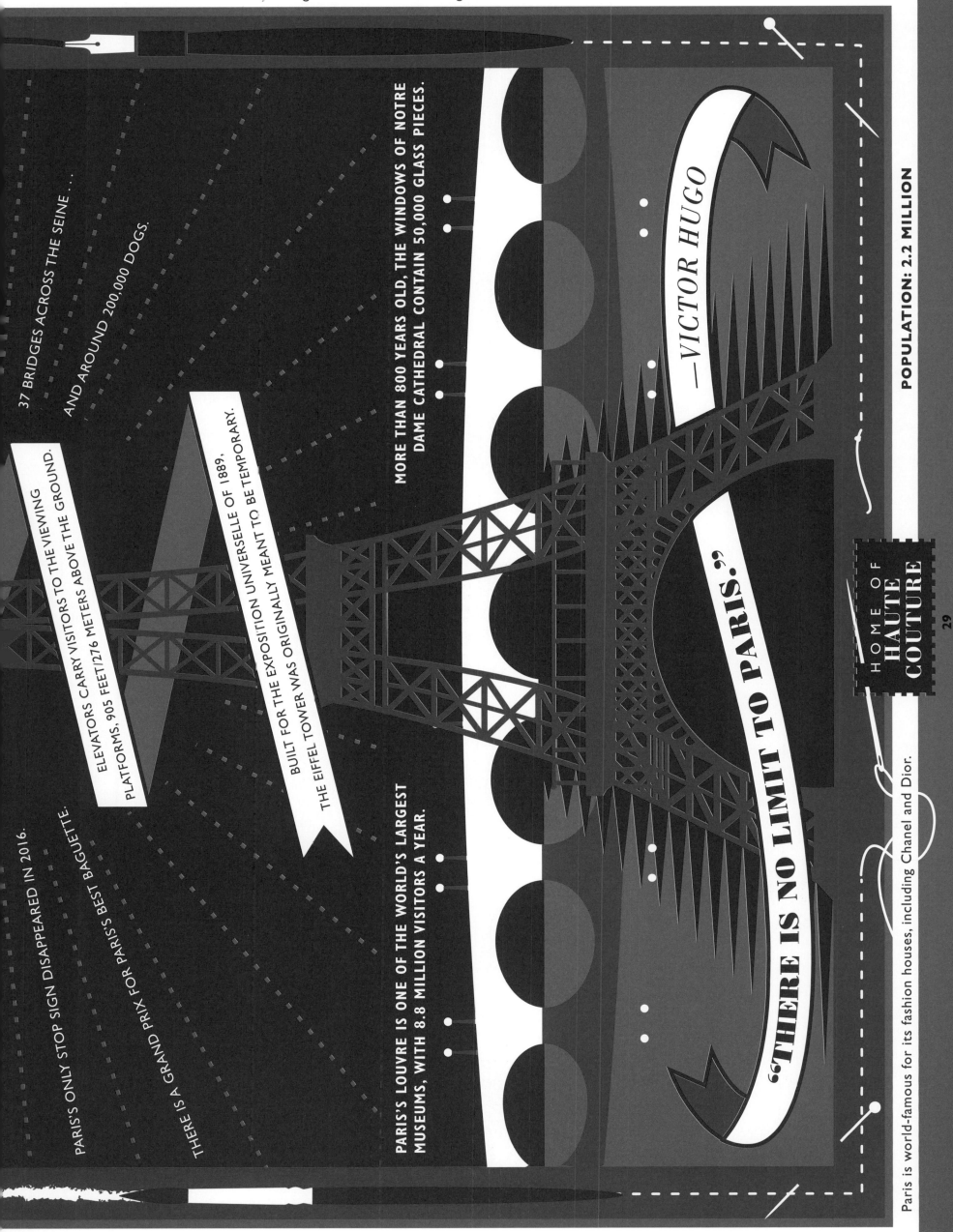

37 BRIDGES ACROSS THE SEINE . . . .

. . . AND AROUND 200,000 DOGS.

ELEVATORS CARRY VISITORS TO THE VIEWING PLATFORMS, 905 FEET/276 METERS ABOVE THE GROUND.

BUILT FOR THE EXPOSITION UNIVERSELLE OF 1889, THE EIFFEL TOWER WAS ORIGINALLY MEANT TO BE TEMPORARY.

MORE THAN 800 YEARS OLD, THE WINDOWS OF NOTRE DAME CATHEDRAL CONTAIN 50,000 GLASS PIECES.

—VICTOR HUGO

"THERE IS NO LIMIT TO PARIS."

PARIS'S ONLY STOP SIGN DISAPPEARED IN 2016.

THERE IS A GRAND PRIX FOR PARIS'S BEST BAGUETTE.

PARIS'S LOUVRE IS ONE OF THE WORLD'S LARGEST MUSEUMS, WITH 8.8 MILLION VISITORS A YEAR.

POPULATION: 2.2 MILLION

HOME OF HAUTE COUTURE

Paris is world-famous for its fashion houses, including Chanel and Dior.

Paris has been home to many famous artists, including Renoir, Rodin, Picasso, Monet, and Manet.

VENICE

Venice has one of the narrowest streets in the world: Calletta, or Ramo Varisco, is only 21 inches/53 centimeters wide in parts.

Venice has been a powerful, prosperous city for more than a thousand years and was its own city-state from the eighth century to the eighteenth.

"Every time I describe a city, I am saying something about Venice." —Italo Calvino

The S-shaped Grand Canal is the biggest canal in Venice and splits the city in two.

Venice is a labyrinth of narrow streets and canals lined with beautiful palaces.

The Rialto Bridge, completed in 1591, is the oldest of the four bridges spanning the Grand Canal.

It is single span, which means it is anchored at each end and there is no support in the middle. At the time, many thought it would crumble under the weight of the marble.

Canals: 177
Palaces: 200
Squares: 127
Gondolas: 400
Gondoliers: 400
Chimneys: 7,000
Bridges: More than 400

The city's name comes from the ancient Veneti people, who lived in the region in the tenth century BCE.

The profession of gondolier is controlled by a guild. To become a gondolier, a person must work first as an apprentice and then pass a rigorous exam.

POPULATION: 271,000

Venice is sinking at an average rate of 1 to 2 millimeters per year, as its soft ground is compacted by the weight of the city's buildings. Acqua alta (high water) is the term for the flooding that occurs as a result of high tides and strong winds in the Venetian lagoon.

31

Venice's central square, Piazza San Marco, is considered one of the finest squares in the world. It is surrounded by a palace, a bell tower, and the famous church Saint Mark's Basilica, known for the four bronze horses on its facade.

Venice is an island city—it is spread over a group of 117 small islands, linked by canals and bridges.

There are six main districts, called sestieri. The most famous is San Marco, which contains the opulent Saint Mark's Basilica, the Doge's Palace, and the 322-foot-/98-meter-high Campanile bell tower.

The Biennale, a major international contemporary art show, takes place in Venice every two years.

The shogun defended his rule using samurai, warriors famed for their prowess in sword fighting, archery, and horse riding.

Tokyo was originally called Edo, meaning "estuary." The city first began to flourish after a military government, the Tokugawa shogunate, was established there in 1603.

GREATER TOKYO IS THE WORLD'S LARGEST METROPOLITAN AREA.

TOKYO

Greater Tokyo includes a number of small outlying islands, some as far as 1,150 miles/1,850 kilometers from the city center.

Mount Fuji, a snowcapped active volcano that lies 60 miles/97 kilometers southwest of the city. On a clear day in Tokyo, it is possible to see

"A CITY DEVOTED TO THE NEW . . . . A POSTMODERN SCIENCE-FICTION STORY SET TEN MINUTES IN THE FUTURE."

— DAVID RAKOFF

The emperor of Japan lives in the Imperial Palace in a large, park-like area in Tokyo, surrounded by a moat and walls.

Koishikawa Korakuen is a traditional Japanese garden that re-creates famous landscapes in miniature, using hills, ponds, trees, and stones.

Buddhism was introduced to Japan in 552 CE, when the king of Baekje (in what is now Korea) sent a mission there that included Buddhist monks and nuns with Buddhist texts and an image of Buddha.

Shinto is Japan's other main religion, alongside Buddhism. It involves devotion to invisible spiritual beings and powers called *kami*. Shrines, often within the home, are the main places of worship.

For two weeks in every year, Tokyo is covered in pink blossoms from its cherry trees, of which Tokyo's Ueno Park has more than 1,000.

At 1,092 feet/332.9 meters, Tokyo Tower (right), inspired by the Eiffel Tower, is the second tallest structure in Japan, while the 2,080-foot-/634-meter-high Tokyo Skytree (left) is the second tallest in the world.

Rainbow Bridge, a half-mile-/798-meter-long suspension bridge across Tokyo Bay, is lit up red, white, and green every night using solar energy stored during the day.

The Tsukiji Fish Market in central Tokyo is the biggest wholesale fish and seafood market in the world.

Shibuya Crossing is the world's busiest pedestrian crossing. At peak times, thousands of pedestrians pass at once from five different directions.

Dubai is located on the southeast coast of the Persian Gulf and is the capital of the Emirate of Dubai.

Dubai is also one of the most expensive cities in the world.

Dubai is the leading commercial center in the Middle East,

A popular tourist destination and business center in the Middle East

DUBAI

THE FASTEST-GROWING CITY ON EARTH

Dubai has more buildings that reach above 980 feet/300 meters and 650 feet/200 meters than any other city in the world. Since 2010, it also has the world's tallest skyline.

Dubai is famous for its skyscrapers, including the world's tallest building — the Burj Khalifa — which stands 2,722 feet/ 829.8 meters high.

After oil was discovered in Dubai in 1966, foreign workers flocked to the city. By 1975, the city's population had grown by more than 300 percent.

Dubai is a member of the United Arab Emirates (UAE), a federation of seven states in the Middle East.

Each state, or emirate, is governed by an absolute monarch.

Dubai Creek is a natural saltwater creek that runs through the heart of the city.

BETWEEN THE FIFTH AND SEVENTH CENTURIES CE, THE COASTAL AREA OF DUBAI WAS KNOWN FOR ITS FISHING, BOAT BUILDING, AND PEARLING. THE PEARL INDUSTRY CONTINUED UNTIL THE 1930S.

Dubai has a hot desert climate, with temperatures reaching highs of 104°F/40°C.

POPULATION: 2.5 MILLION

Dubai has its own archipelago of artificial islands, including one in the shape of a palm tree that has more than 500 homes and 28 hotels.

At 775,000 square feet/72,000 square meters, Dubai Miracle Garden is the world's largest flower garden, with a total of 109 million flowers.

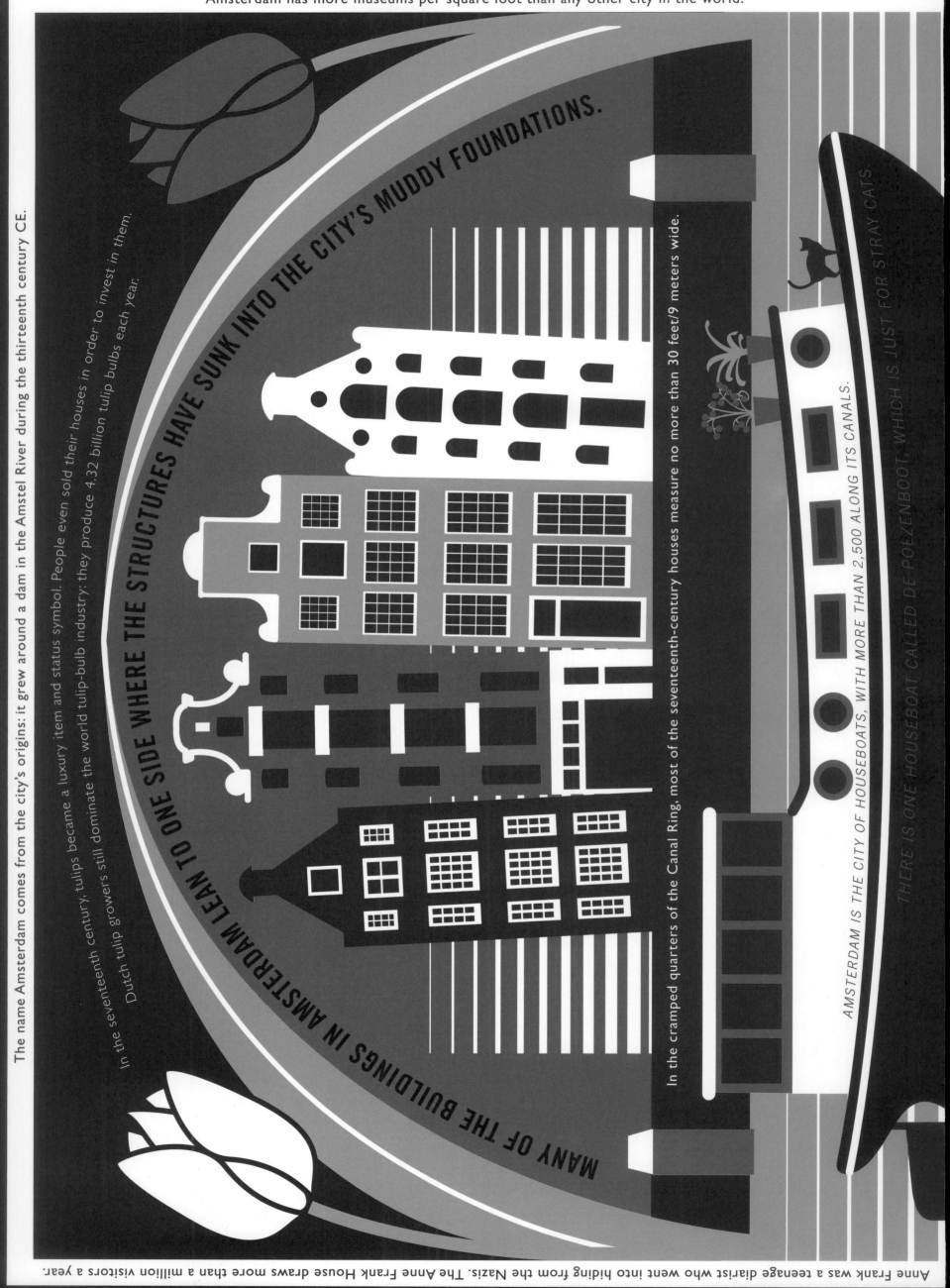

The name Amsterdam comes from the city's origins: it grew around a dam in the Amstel River during the thirteenth century CE.

In the seventeenth century, tulips became a luxury item and status symbol. People even sold their houses in order to invest in them.

Dutch tulip growers still dominate the world tulip-bulb industry: they produce 4.32 billion tulip bulbs each year.

MANY OF THE BUILDINGS IN AMSTERDAM LEAN TO ONE SIDE WHERE THE STRUCTURES HAVE SUNK INTO THE CITY'S MUDDY FOUNDATIONS.

In the cramped quarters of the Canal Ring, most of the seventeenth-century houses measure no more than 30 feet/9 meters wide.

AMSTERDAM IS THE CITY OF HOUSEBOATS, WITH MORE THAN 2,500 ALONG ITS CANALS.

THERE IS ONE HOUSEBOAT CALLED DE POEZENBOOT, WHICH IS JUST FOR STRAY CATS.

The Rijksmuseum houses some of the greatest Dutch artworks, including Vermeer's *The Milkmaid* and Rembrandt's *The Night Watch*.

AMSTERDAM

Diamond factories: 10+
Bicycles: 880,000+
Bridges: 1,281
Canals: 165

UP TO 15,000 BICYCLE WRECKS ARE FISHED OUT OF THE CANALS PER YEAR.

AMSTERDAM IS SOMETIMES CALLED THE "VENICE OF THE NORTH," AS IT HAS ALMOST AS MANY CANALS AS VENICE, AND MORE BRIDGES.

MOKUM*

*Amsterdam's nickname, Mokum, means "place" or "safe haven" in Hebrew.

FROM 1585 TO 1672, IN A TIME KNOWN AS THE GOLDEN AGE, AMSTERDAM WAS AT THE CENTER OF THE WORLD'S ECONOMY.

POPULATION: 814,000

Amsterdam is the Netherlands' largest and most visited city, with more than 8 million visitors per year.

Amsterdam is known for its heavy hitters of art history: Rembrandt, Vermeer, and Van Gogh.

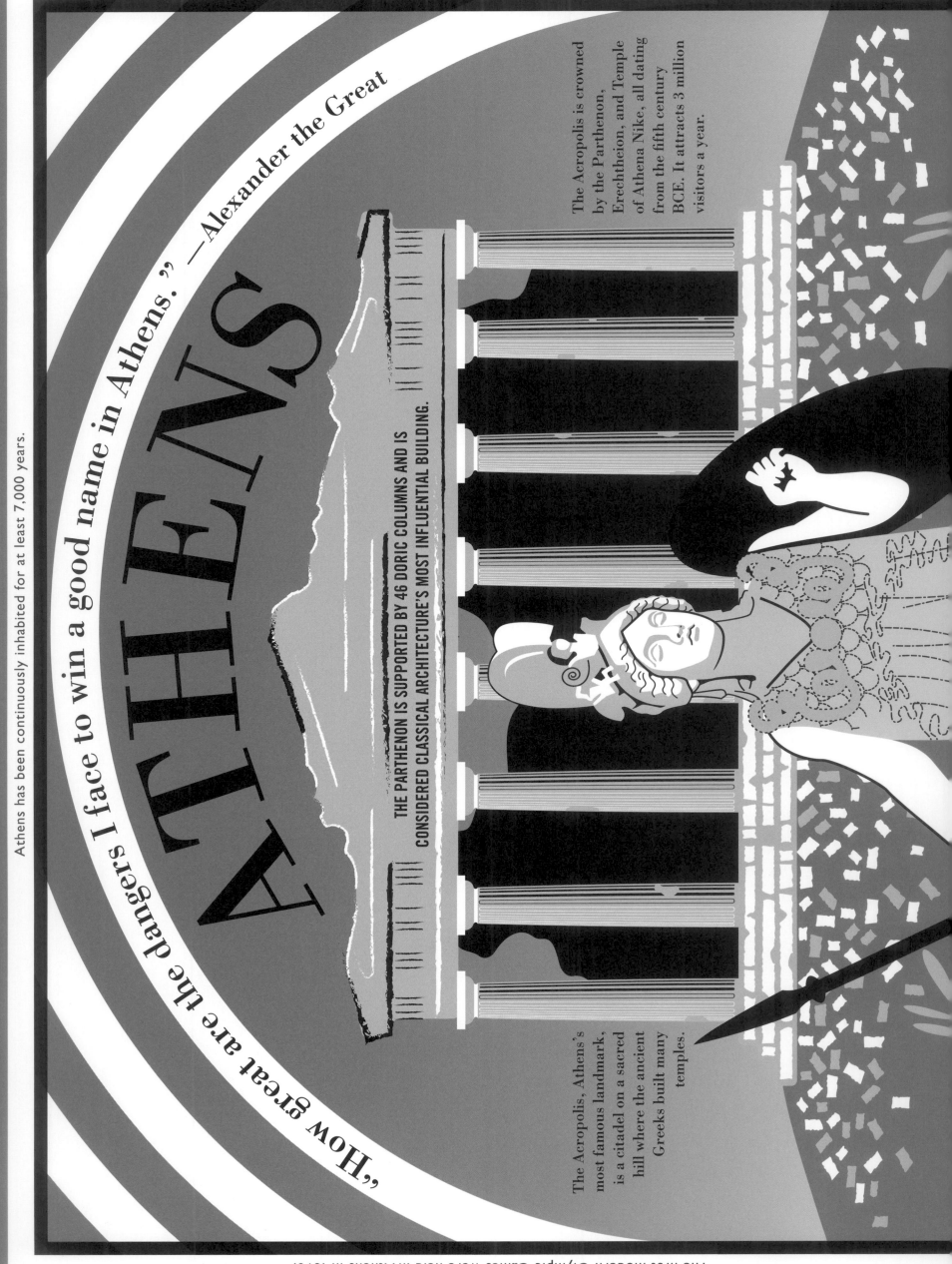

ATHENS

"How great are the dangers I face to win a good name in Athens." —Alexander the Great

Athens has been continuously inhabited for at least 7,000 years.

THE PARTHENON IS SUPPORTED BY 46 DORIC COLUMNS AND IS CONSIDERED CLASSICAL ARCHITECTURE'S MOST INFLUENTIAL BUILDING.

The Acropolis is crowned by the Parthenon, Erechtheion, and Temple of Athena Nike, all dating from the fifth century BCE. It attracts 3 million visitors a year.

The Acropolis, Athens's most famous landmark, is a citadel on a sacred hill where the ancient Greeks built many temples.

THE CRADLE OF WESTERN CIVILIZATION AND THE BIRTHPLACE OF DEMOCRACY

During the Golden Age of Democracy (480–404 BCE), Athens was home to playwrights Aeschylus, Sophocles, and Euripides, historians Herodotus and Thucydides, and the physician Hippocrates.

Athens spreads across the central plain of Attica and is bounded by four mountains: Mount Parnitha, Mount Pentelikon, Mount Aigaleo, and Mount Hymettus.

Athens is named after the goddess Athena. The Parthenon was built in her honor.

At 900 feet/296 meters, Mount Lycabettus is Athens's highest point. From its peak, you can see from the Acropolis to the Temple of Zeus.

In 1834, when Athens was chosen as the capital of Greece, it was just a small town built around the foot of the Acropolis.

POPULATION: 665,000

Built into the hillside below the Acropolis, Plaka is Athens's oldest residential quarter.

The Odeon, a stone theater on the southwest slope of the Acropolis, was built in 161 CE by Herodes Atticus in memory of his wife.

Athens is served by Piraeus, the largest passenger port in Europe.

Delhi has intensely hot summers lasting from April to June, with maximum temperatures of 117°F/47°C.

In the early 1900s, British architects Sir Edwin Lutyens and Sir Herbert Baker built New Delhi to be Britain's imperial capital of India. The foundation stones were laid by King George V and Queen Mary on December 15, 1911.

The city of Delhi is made up of Old Delhi, in the north, which is the historic city, and New Delhi, in the south, which is the capital of India. During the 1800s, British colonial forces seized Delhi and remained in power until Indian independence in 1947.

DELHI

The Quṭb Mīnār is a 240-foot-/73-meter-high tower of victory, built by Quṭb al-Dīn Aibak, the sultan of Quṭb, in 1193.

The Red Fort, built by Shah Jahan in 1648 in the center of Old Delhi, was the residence of Mughal emperors for nearly 200 years.

Many different types of monkeys live in Delhi. Hindus consider monkeys to be the living representatives of the god Hanuman, and tradition calls for feeding monkeys on Tuesdays and Saturdays.

According to one popular legend, the city was named for Raja Dhilu, a king who was said to have founded the city in 800 BCE.

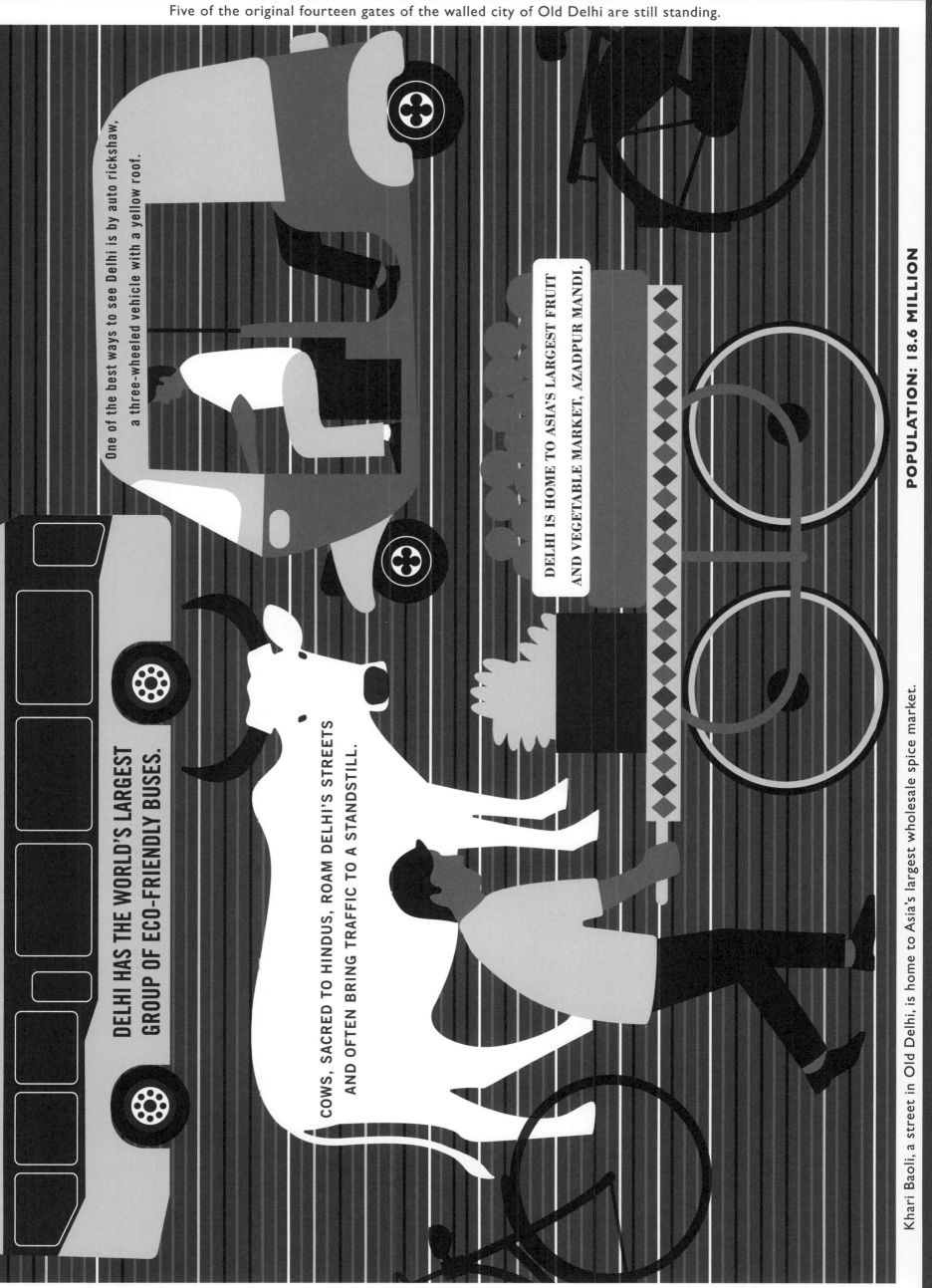

One of the best ways to see Delhi is by auto rickshaw, a three-wheeled vehicle with a yellow roof.

DELHI IS HOME TO ASIA'S LARGEST FRUIT AND VEGETABLE MARKET, AZADPUR MANDI.

DELHI HAS THE WORLD'S LARGEST GROUP OF ECO-FRIENDLY BUSES.

COWS, SACRED TO HINDUS, ROAM DELHI'S STREETS AND OFTEN BRING TRAFFIC TO A STANDSTILL.

POPULATION: 18.6 MILLION

Khari Baoli, a street in Old Delhi, is home to Asia's largest wholesale spice market.

Beijing is famous for its *siheyuan*: residences that surround and share a common courtyard.

There are remnants of the Great Wall of China in the mountains to the north of the city.

BEIJING

LOCATED IN NORTHERN CHINA, BEIJING IS CHINA'S CAPITAL.

Bei means "northern," and *jing* means "capital," so Beijing means "northern capital."

ONLY THE EMPEROR, HIS IMMEDIATE FAMILY, AND THEIR SERVANTS WERE ALLOWED TO ENTER THE FORBIDDEN CITY.

THE TEMPLE OF HEAVEN IS A FAMOUS TEMPLE WHERE MING AND QING EMPERORS WOULD WORSHIP AND PRAY TO THE GODS AND THEIR ANCESTORS.

BETWEEN 1420 AND 1911, 24 EMPERORS OF THE MING AND QING DYNASTIES OCCUPIED A PALACE COMPLEX CALLED THE FORBIDDEN CITY.

The city is known for its opulent palaces, temples, parks, gardens, tombs, walls, and gates.

Fuling jiabing is a popular traditional Beijing snack made from *fu ling*, a fungus used in traditional Chinese medicine.

BEIJING'S HISTORY BEGAN MORE THAN 3,000 YEARS AGO; IT HAS BEEN CHINA'S CENTER OF GOVERNMENT FOR ALMOST 800 YEARS. BEIJING WAS FORMERLY ROMANIZED AS "PEKING"; ITS OTHER NAMES HAVE INCLUDED BEIPING AND DADU.

POPULATION: 21.7 MILLION

AT 4.7 MILLION SQUARE FEET/440,000 SQUARE METERS, TIANANMEN SQUARE IS ONE OF THE WORLD'S LARGEST CITY SQUARES.

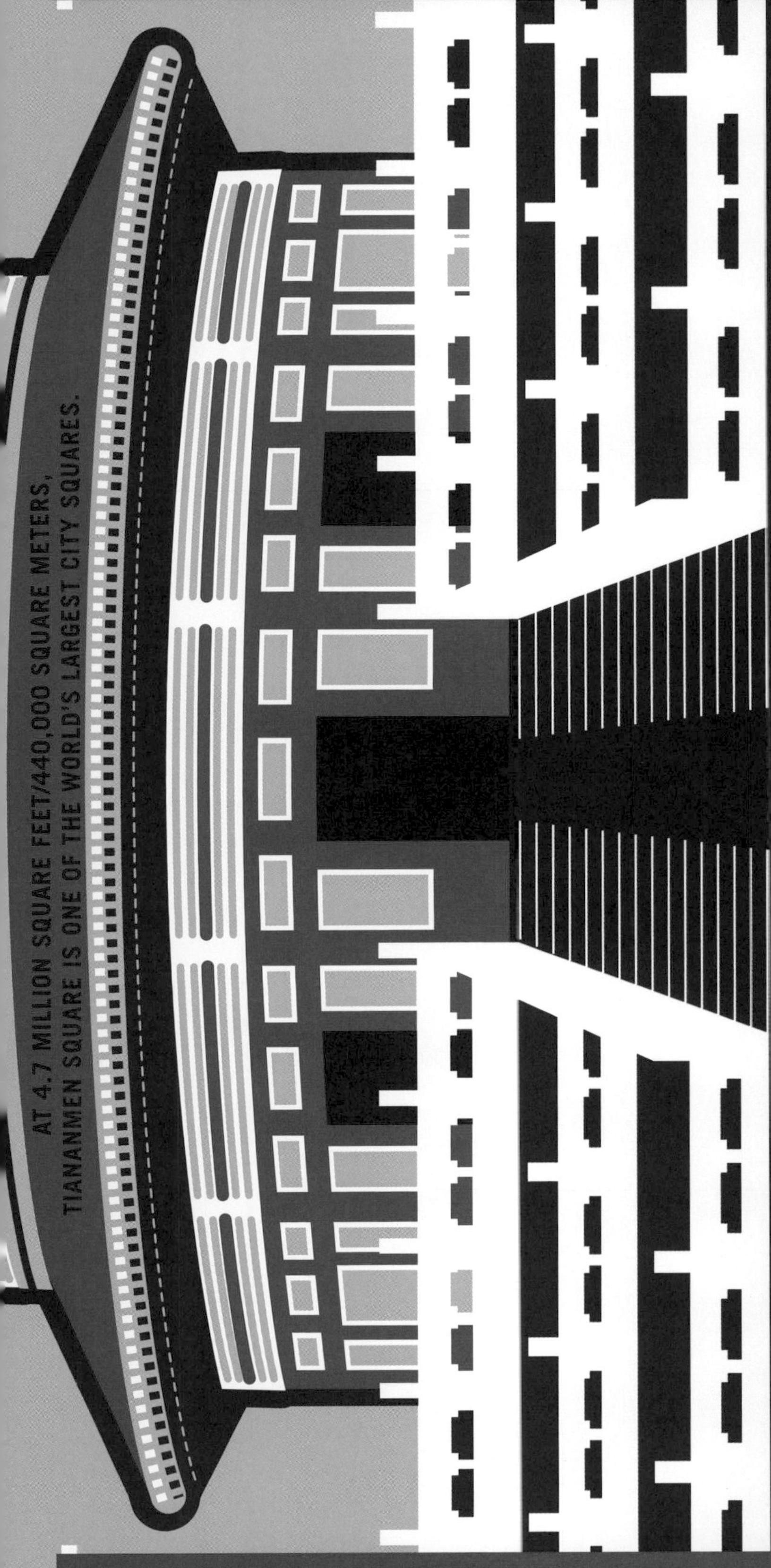

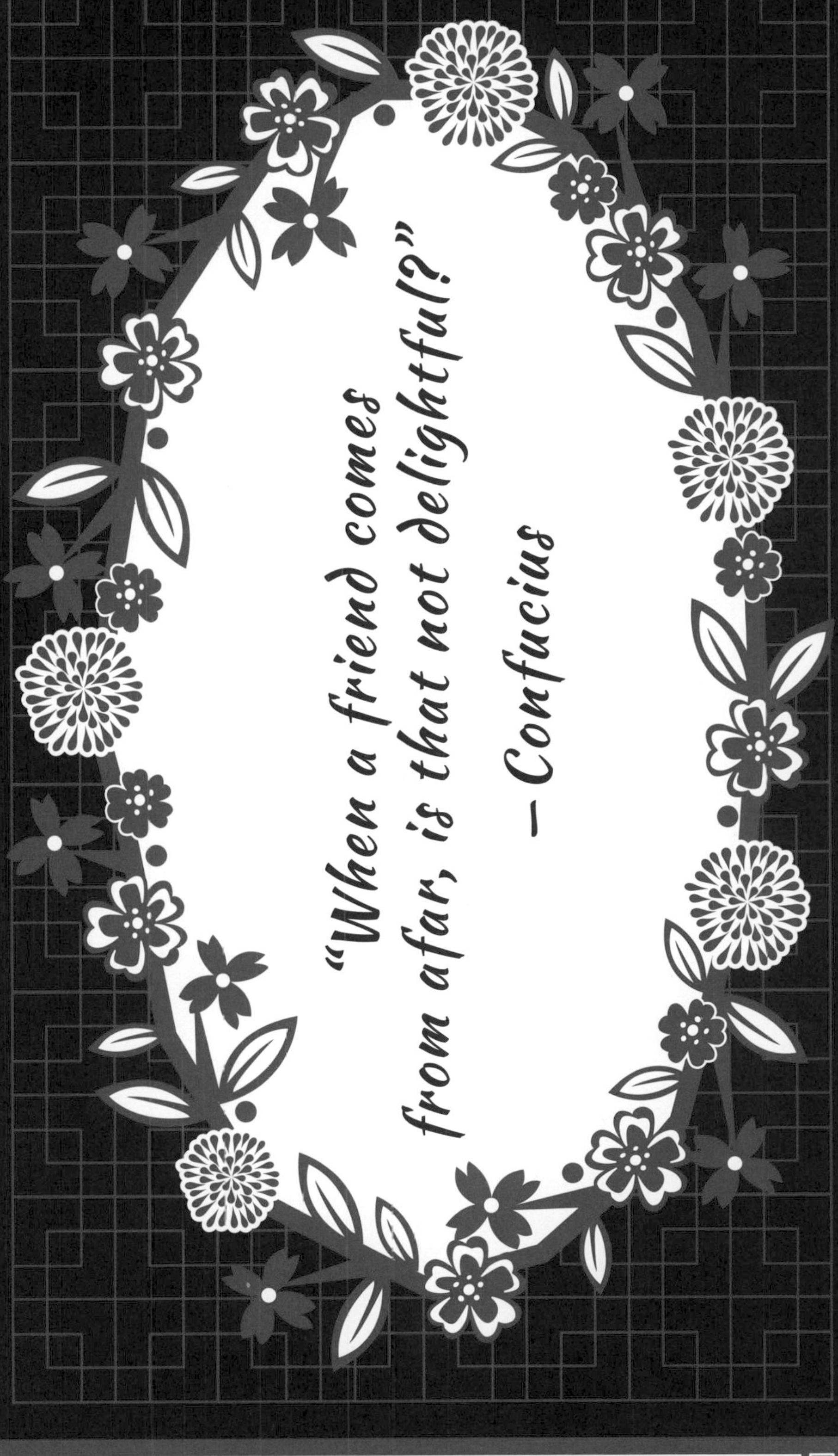

"When a friend comes from afar, is that not delightful?"
—Confucius

The Chinese rose and the chrysanthemum are Beijing's official flowers.

THE PEKING MAN, THE OLDEST EVIDENCE OF HUMAN HABITATION IN THE BEIJING AREA, WAS FOUND IN THE CAVES OF DRAGON BONE HILL AND DATES TO AROUND 700,000 YEARS AGO.

Beijing's most popular dishes include hot and sour soup, moo shu pork, and Peking duck.

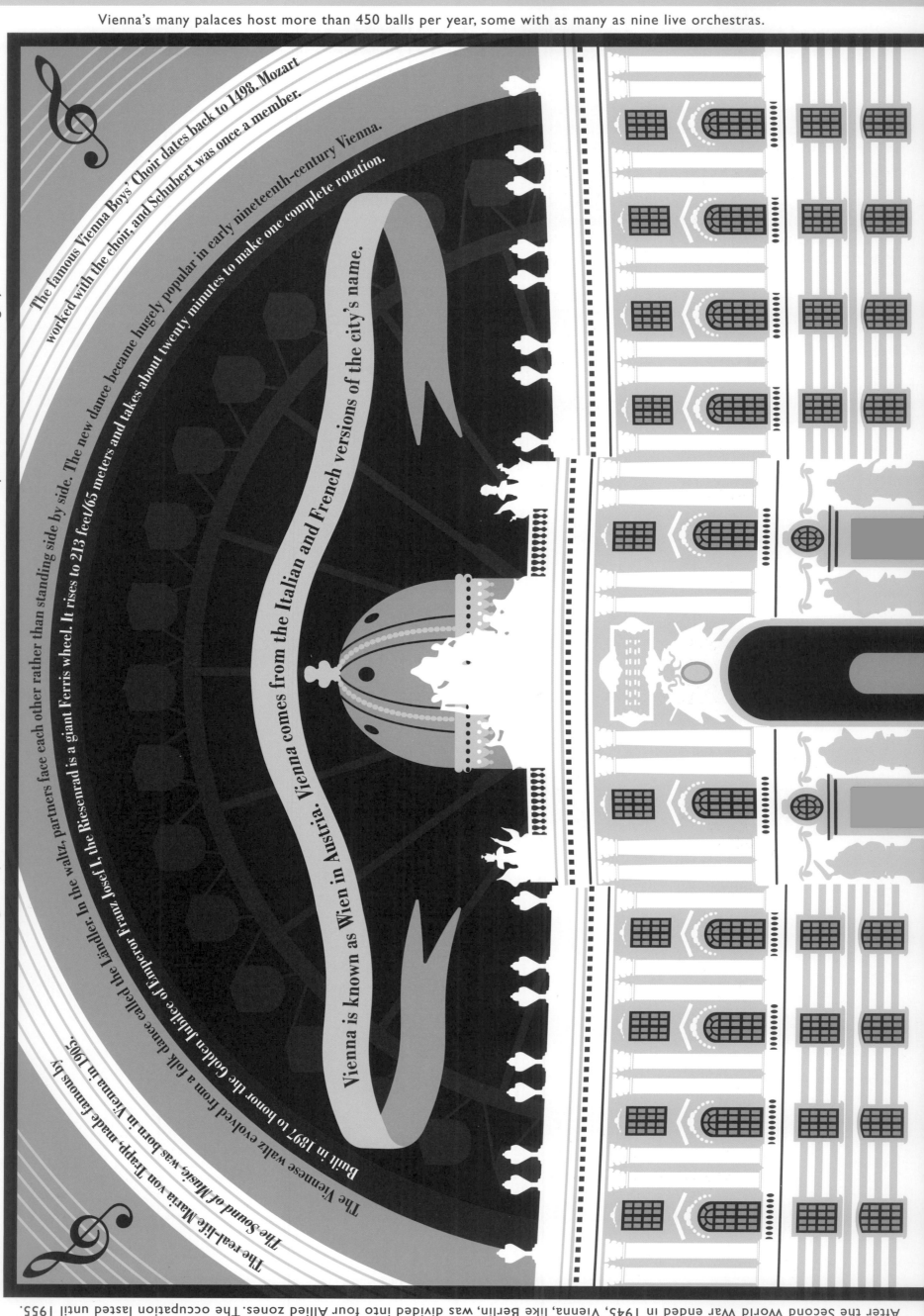

Vienna is the capital of and largest city in Austria, located close to the borders of the Czech Republic, Slovakia, and Hungary.

The famous Vienna Boys' Choir dates back to 1498. Mozart worked with the choir, and Schubert was once a member.

The new dance became hugely popular in early nineteenth-century Vienna.

In the waltz, partners face each other rather than standing side by side.

It rises to 213 feet/65 meters and takes about twenty minutes to make one complete rotation.

Built in 1897 to honor the Golden Jubilee of Emperor Franz Josef 1, the Riesenrad is a giant Ferris wheel.

The Viennese waltz evolved from a folk dance called the Ländler.

Vienna comes from the Italian and French versions of the city's name. Vienna is known as Wien in Austria.

The Sound of Music.

The real-life Maria von Trapp, made famous by

was born in Vienna in 1905.

VIENNA

POPULATION: 1.8 MILLION

The vast Hofburg was the home of the Habsburgs from 1273 to 1918, with new rulers adding further sections. It is now the Austrian president's offices.

The oldest section of the Hofburg is the thirteenth-century Schweizerhof ("Swiss Courtyard"), named after the Swiss guards who used to protect it.

For more than 450 years, the Spanish Riding School in Vienna has practiced classical dressage using the famous Lipizzan horses, a breed that dates back to the sixteenth century.

The riding school is the oldest of its kind. It was first based in a wooden arena at the Josefsplatz, but in 1729 Emperor Charles VI commissioned the white riding hall that is still used today.

The horses are taught to make controlled, stylized jumps as well as movements known as the half-pass, counter-canter, flying change, pirouette, passage, and piaffe.

VIENNA IS OFTEN CALLED THE CITY OF MUSIC BECAUSE OF ITS LONG HISTORY AS A SOURCE OF WORLD-CLASS MUSIC. MORE FAMOUS COMPOSERS HAVE LIVED AND WORKED IN VIENNA THAN IN ANY OTHER CITY, INCLUDING MOZART, HAYDN, BEETHOVEN, SCHUBERT, BRAHMS, AND MAHLER.

45

Famous visitors to Griechenbeisl, Vienna's oldest restaurant, have included Beethoven, Brahms, Schubert, and Mark Twain.

A popular treat in Vienna is Sacher torte, a rich chocolate cake with apricot jam filling, once favored by Emperor Franz Josef.

The main pyramids in Teotihuacan were the Pyramids of the Sun and Moon. The Pyramid of the Sun was the largest, reaching nearly 250 feet/75 meters high.

Mexico City is located in the Valley of Mexico, a large valley in the high plateaus of south-central Mexico, at an altitude of around 7,200 feet/2,200 meters.

The ancient and holy city of Teotihuacan, meaning "the place where the gods were created," lies around 30 miles/50 kilometers northeast of Mexico City.

Within the city walls of Tenochtitlán, there were palaces, pyramids, and temples to the Aztec gods, who were worshipped with human sacrifices.

Mexico City was originally named Tenochtitlán and was built in 1325 by the Aztecs, a fierce tribe of warriors who settled in the Valley of Mexico in the thirteenth century.

MEXICO CITY

Tenochtitlán was the Aztecs' capital city and became the center of their powerful empire, which reached across large parts of Mexico and Central America.

Every night, competing mariachi bands gather in the city's Plaza Garibaldi, wearing silver-spangled outfits and sombreros. Groups are usually made up of two or four violinists, three trumpeters, three or four men on guitars, and a vocalist belting out ballads.

The palace was eventually completed in 1934. Huge murals by famous Mexican artists adorn its walls. It stages art exhibitions, literature events, and opera and ballet performances and is known as the "Cathedral of Art in Mexico."

Frida Kahlo is one of Mexico's most famous artists. She lived and died in La Casa Azul (the Blue House), along with her husband, fellow artist Diego Rivera. The house is now an art gallery and museum and attracts around 25,000 visitors each month.

The Palacio de Bellas Artes ("Palace of Fine Arts") is an opulent, white marble palace, built in the neoclassical, art nouveau, and art deco styles. Building ceased during the Mexican Revolution (1910–1920).

PALACIO DE BELLAS ARTES

POPULATION: 8.9 MILLION

Mexico's Day of the Dead dates back to the Aztec period. Celebrants believe that the spirits of the dead return for a visit.

In 1985, an earthquake with a magnitude of 8.0 hit the city. At least 9,500 people were killed and 3,000 buildings seriously damaged.

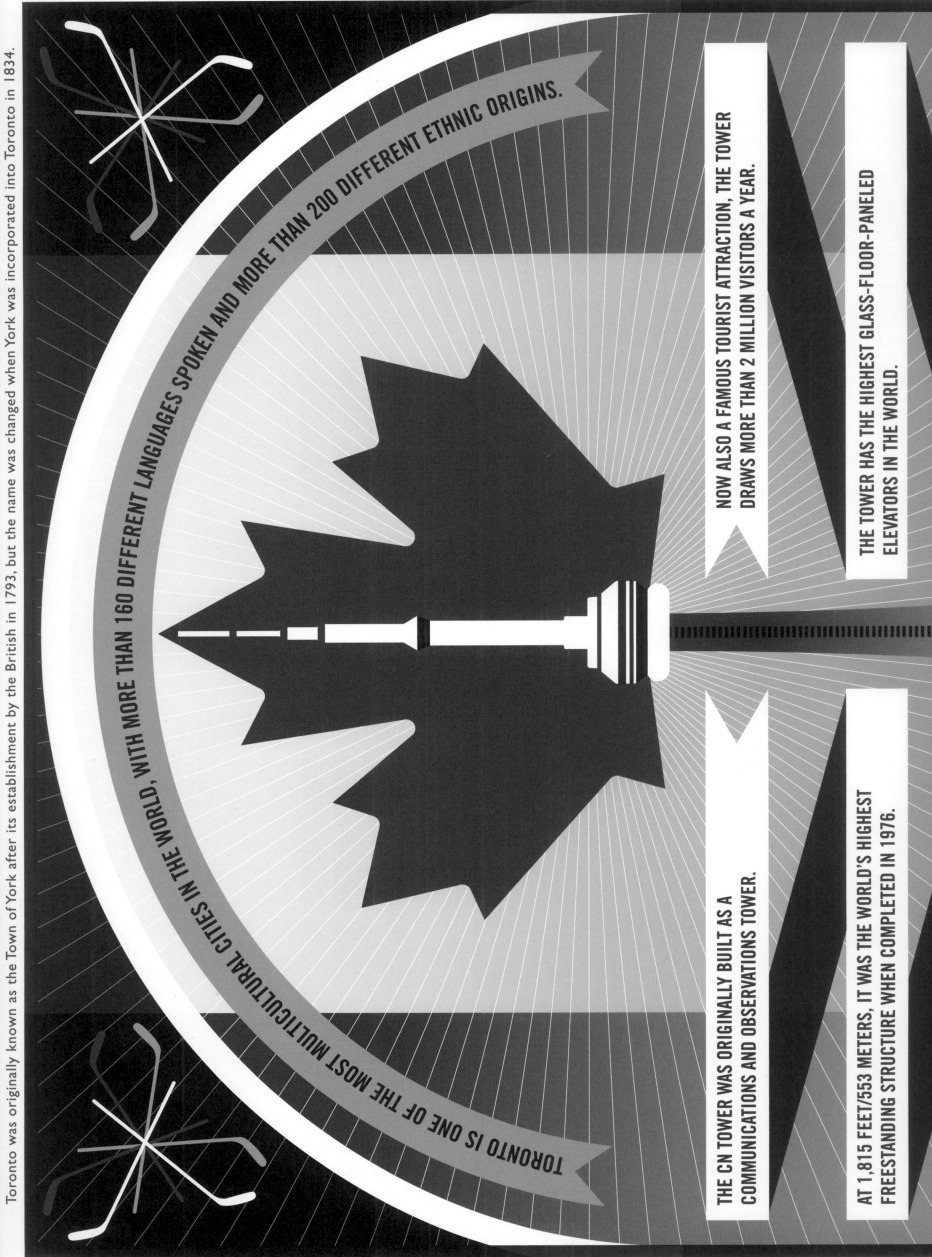

Toronto was originally known as the Town of York after its establishment by the British in 1793, but the name was changed when York was incorporated into Toronto in 1834.

TORONTO IS ONE OF THE MOST MULTICULTURAL CITIES IN THE WORLD, WITH MORE THAN 160 DIFFERENT LANGUAGES SPOKEN AND MORE THAN 200 DIFFERENT ETHNIC ORIGINS.

NOW ALSO A FAMOUS TOURIST ATTRACTION, THE TOWER DRAWS MORE THAN 2 MILLION VISITORS A YEAR.

THE TOWER HAS THE HIGHEST GLASS-FLOOR-PANELED ELEVATORS IN THE WORLD.

THE CN TOWER WAS ORIGINALLY BUILT AS A COMMUNICATIONS AND OBSERVATIONS TOWER.

AT 1,815 FEET/553 METERS, IT WAS THE WORLD'S HIGHEST FREESTANDING STRUCTURE WHEN COMPLETED IN 1976.

The Royal Ontario Museum is one of the largest museums in North America, with more than 6 million specimens and artifacts.

TORONTO

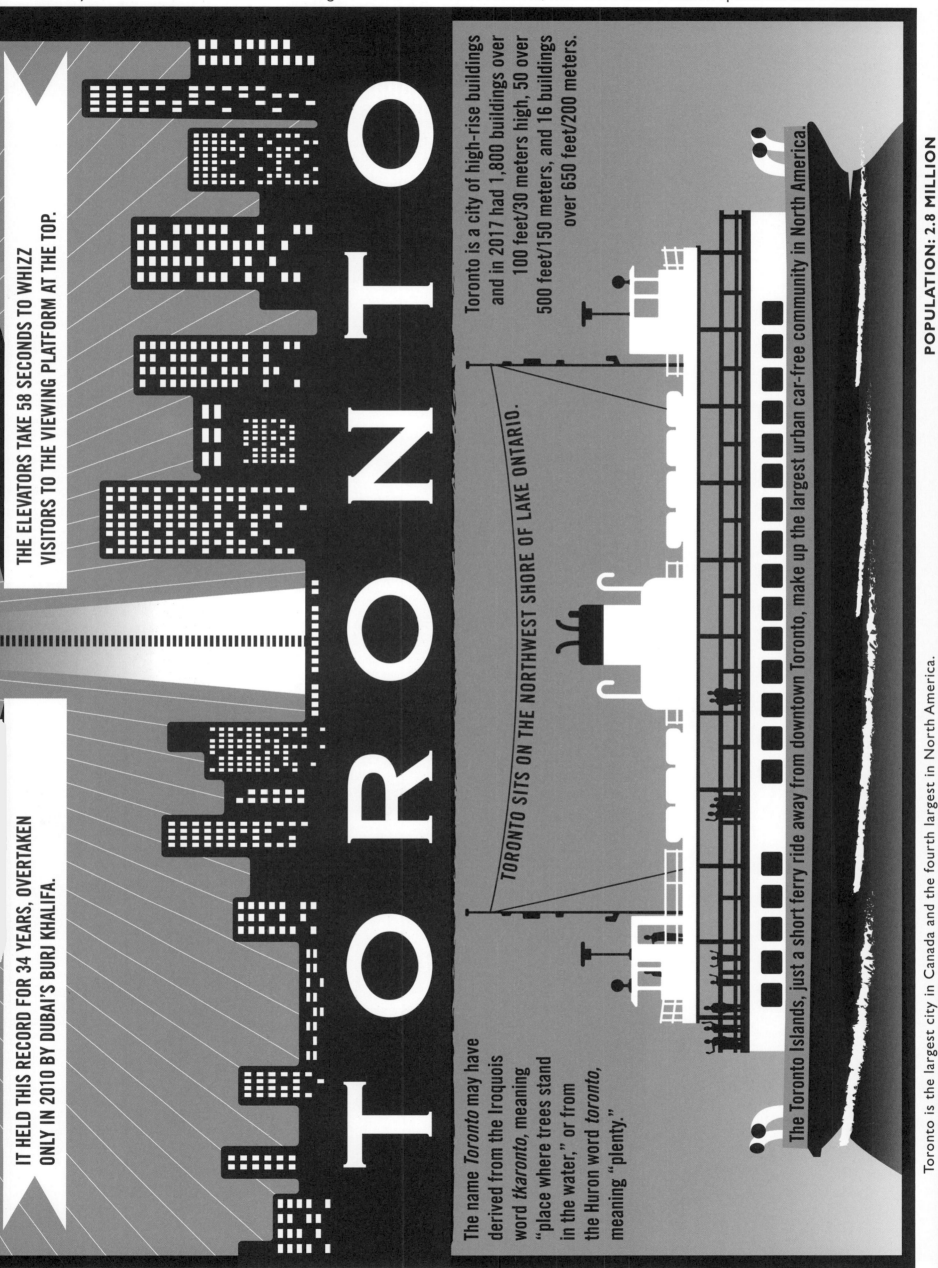

IT HELD THIS RECORD FOR 34 YEARS, OVERTAKEN ONLY IN 2010 BY DUBAI'S BURJ KHALIFA.

THE ELEVATORS TAKE 58 SECONDS TO WHIZZ VISITORS TO THE VIEWING PLATFORM AT THE TOP.

Toronto is a city of high-rise buildings and in 2017 had 1,800 buildings over 100 feet/30 meters high, 50 over 500 feet/150 meters, and 16 buildings over 650 feet/200 meters.

TORONTO SITS ON THE NORTHWEST SHORE OF LAKE ONTARIO.

The name *Toronto* may have derived from the Iroquois word *tkaronto*, meaning "place where trees stand in the water," or from the Huron word *toronto*, meaning "plenty."

The Toronto Islands, just a short ferry ride away from downtown Toronto, make up the largest urban car-free community in North America.

POPULATION: 2.8 MILLION

Toronto is the largest city in Canada and the fourth largest in North America.

The Wendat (Huron) people inhabited the Toronto region for thousands of years, followed by the Iroquois.

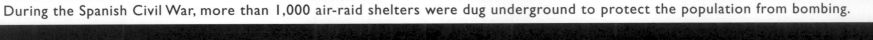

During the Spanish Civil War, more than 1,000 air-raid shelters were dug underground to protect the population from bombing.

Barcelona is the capital of Spain's Catalonia region. Both Catalan and Spanish are official languages in Barcelona.

Gaudí's original design for the Sagrada Família had eighteen spires, of which only eight have been built so far.

The Sagrada Família's tallest spire will be 560 feet/170 meters high — intended to be 3 feet/1 meter shorter than Montjuïc hill in Barcelona, as Gaudí believed that nothing human-made should be "higher than God's work."

The largest city on the Mediterranean coastline

Barcelona is known for the work of the architect Antoni Gaudí. His most famous building is the Sagrada Família, a huge basilica begun in 1882 and still under construction.

Gaudí devoted his last years to the project and is buried in the crypt there. At the time of his death, at the age of 73, the church was only a quarter complete.

Romans arrived in the area in 218 BCE and founded a settlement called Barcino on the site that would become the medieval city.

BARCELONA

POPULATION: 1.7 MILLION

The Sagrada Família has taken more than 100 years to build. Its proposed completion date is 2026, 100 years after Gaudí's death.

Casa Milà, another of Gaudí's creations, is also known as La Pedrera, or "the stone quarry," for its rough-hewn gray stone facade.

The Port of Barcelona is Europe's largest cruise port, with approximately 2.6 million cruisers passing through each year.

In 1999, Barcelona became the first and only city to receive a Royal Gold Medal for architecture from the Royal Institute of British Architects.

A series of beaches stretch across Barcelona's 2-mile/4.5-kilometer coastline. Six were created especially for the 1992 Olympic Games.

51

Catalonia has a tradition, dating back to the eighteenth century, of building human towers known as *castells*.

Cairo is located in northern Egypt, along the banks of the Nile River — traditionally considered the world's longest river.

Cairo is the capital and largest city of Egypt. Along with the surrounding districts, it makes up the largest metropolitan area in the Middle East.

The Great Pyramid is the oldest of the Seven Wonders of the Ancient World.

largest of them, the Great Pyramid is made from roughly 2.3 million limestone blocks, each weighing around 2¼ tons/2 metric tons.

Built circa 2500 BCE, the

lie the Pyramids of Giza. Built circa 2500 BCE, the

Southwest of Cairo, visible on the skyline, lie the world's tallest human-made structure for nearly 4,000 years. It is

The Great Pyramid was the world's tallest human-made structure for nearly 4,000 years. It is

CAIRO

CITY OF A THOUSAND MINARETS

& MOTHER OF THE WORLD

Cairo was first founded in 969 CE by the Fatimids. It was created as a royal enclosure for the ruling caliph.

The area around Cairo's old walled city has hundreds of mosques, madrasas, and fortifications. The area is famous for its historic monuments and examples of Islamic architecture.

The eastern edge of Cairo is known as the City of the Dead, made up of many cemeteries and elaborate tombs. Today it is a densely populated area where many people live and work in overcrowded conditions.

People from Cairo are called Cairenes.

The Egyptian Museum houses more than 100,000 ancient Egyptian antiquities, including finds from Tutankhamen's tomb, including his death mask, lion throne, and nested sarcophagi.

The maze-like market Khān al-Khalīlī was first built in the fourteenth century. It is now a huge assortment of shops, surrounded by markets selling gold, copper pots, textiles, rugs, and spices.

Cairo is a city of contrasts. Old Cairo is crowded with minarets and ancient churches, while modern Cairo has high-rise offices, hotels along the Nile, and four-lane highways.

POPULATION: 12 MILLION

Cairo's 6th October Bridge took nearly 30 years to build and is the longest bridge in Egypt.

The oldest structure in Cairo is an ancient Roman fortress called Babylon, which was built around 525 BCE.

Parts of present-day Germany, including Berlin, were once part of the Kingdom of Prussia (1701–1918). Many of the city's landmarks date back to that time.

"Ich bin ein Berliner." —John F. Kennedy

Museums: 175
Bridges: 1,700
Theaters: 140

Restaurants: 6,500
Sandwich bars: 2,800
Ice-cream parlors & cafés: 546

The statue at the top of the Brandenburg Gate is called the Quadriga and shows the goddess of victory.

The Brandenburg Gate was commissioned by King Frederick II of Prussia and erected in 1791.

The Holocaust Memorial, near the Brandenburg Gate, covers about 200,000 square feet/19,000 square meters. It is a place of remembrance commemorating the Holocaust, in which 6 million Jewish people died under the orders of the Nazi government.

During the collapse of the Soviet Union, it was announced on November 9, 1989, that people could move freely between East and West Berlin. Much of the Berlin Wall was torn down as people celebrated.

At first, its name was Gate of Peace—but after 1814, it became known as Gate of Victory.

Checkpoint Charlie was the name of the best-known Berlin Wall crossing point from the Cold War period.

From 1961 to 1989, the city was divided by the Berlin Wall, built by the Communist government in East Berlin to keep it separate from West Berlin.

After the Second World War, the Allies divided Berlin into four zones, three of which became West Berlin, in West Germany, and one of which became East Berlin, under Soviet control.

In 1806, Napoléon I's French forces captured and occupied Berlin. Napoleon took the Quadriga back to France as a symbol of his victory. In 1814, Napoléon was defeated and the Quadriga was returned to the Brandenburg Gate.

Berlin has more than 112 miles/180 kilometers of navigable waterways and more bridges than Venice.

BERLIN

POPULATION: 3.5 MILLION

At 1,217 feet/368 meters, the Fernsehturm, a TV tower, is the tallest structure in Germany.

Built in 1895, the double-decker Oberbaum Bridge links two boroughs that were once divided by the Berlin Wall and has become an important symbol of the city's unity.

Berlin is in northeastern Germany, on the banks of the rivers Spree and Havel.

During the Second World War, Berlin was almost completely destroyed. It was subject to 363 air raids by the Allies.

The city flower is the *yulan*, a white flower belonging to the magnolia family that blossoms in spring.

IT HAS THE WORLD'S HIGHEST OBSERVATION DECK WITHIN A BUILDING AND THE WORLD'S FASTEST ELEVATORS, WITH A TOP SPEED OF 46 MILES/74 KILOMETERS PER HOUR.

AT 2,073 FEET/632 METERS, SHANGHAI TOWER, IN THE LUJIAZUI FINANCIAL DISTRICT, IS THE WORLD'S SECOND-TALLEST BUILDING.

THE LARGEST CITY IN THE WORLD

SHANGHAI

Along the Yangtze River

SHANGHAI BOOMED IN THE 1980S, WHEN IT BECAME A LEADING FINANCIAL CENTER AND SKYSCRAPERS SHOT UP ACROSS THE CITY.

Once just a small fishing village, Shanghai developed into one of China's most important trading centers during the Qing dynasty (1644–1912).

The Shanghai dialect, known as Shanghainese, has nearly 14 million speakers.

POPULATION: 24 MILLION

THE JADE BUDDHA TEMPLE WAS BUILT TO HOUSE TWO BUDDHA STATUES THAT WERE BROUGHT FROM BURMA BY A MONK NAMED HUIGEN. THE MAIN FEATURE IS A 6-FOOT-/1.9-METER-HIGH BUDDHA CARVED FROM ONE PIECE OF PURE JADE.

THE SHANGHAI MAGLEV, OR MAGNETIC LEVITATION TRAIN, IS THE FASTEST COMMERCIAL HIGH-SPEED ELECTRIC TRAIN IN THE WORLD. IT TAKES PASSENGERS FROM PUDONG INTERNATIONAL AIRPORT TO THE CITY AT SPEEDS OF UP TO 268 MILES/431 KILOMETERS PER HOUR.

DIRECTLY OPPOSITE THE BUND IS LUJIAZUI, THE NEW FINANCIAL CENTER OF SHANGHAI, FAMOUS FOR ITS SOARING SKYSCRAPERS.

NANJING ROAD, ONE OF THE BUSIEST SHOPPING STREETS IN THE WORLD, RUNS FOR 3½ MILES/5.5 KILOMETERS THROUGH THE CITY.

SHANGHAI MEANS "ABOVE THE SEA." THE CITY WAS NAMED FOR ITS LOCATION AT THE MOUTH OF THE YANGTZE RIVER.

Shanghai lies along a plain in the Yangtze River Delta and is mostly flat, on average only 13 feet/4 meters above sea level.

57

IN THE PAST, PARTS OF SHANGHAI WERE GIVEN TO FOREIGN COUNTRIES AS CONCESSIONS. THE FRENCH CONCESSION, WHICH WAS UNDER FRENCH ADMINISTRATION FROM 1849 TO 1943, IS THE BEST KNOWN AND PRESERVED, AND IS NOW A POPULAR TOURIST DESTINATION.

SHANGHAI IS THE WORLD'S BUSIEST CONTAINER PORT.

THE BUND, A WATERFRONT AREA KNOWN FOR ITS SWEEP OF GRAND BUILDINGS, IS ONE OF SHANGHAI'S MOST ICONIC TOURIST ATTRACTIONS. IN THE 1900s, THESE ART DECO AND NEOCLASSICAL BUILDINGS WERE HOME TO THE CITY'S MOST POWERFUL BANKS AND TRADING HOUSES.

MOTHER CITY

Cape Town was developed by the Dutch East India Company as a supply station for Dutch ships sailing to East Africa, India, and the Far East.

Kirstenbosch National Botanical Garden was the first of its kind in the world. It was founded in 1913 to preserve South Africa's indigenous plants.

TABLE MOUNTAIN, WITH ITS FLAT TOP, WAS FORMED ABOUT 300 MILLION YEARS AGO. TODAY IT IS HOME TO AN ESTIMATED 2,200 PLANT SPECIES, INCLUDING MANY THAT ARE UNIQUE TO THE AREA.

Nelson Mandela was the first black president of South Africa. He had previously spent 27 years in prison for trying to overthrow the pro-apartheid government. The regime treated nonwhite people as second-class citizens and wanted to keep white and nonwhite people separate from each other.

Mandela was held prisoner on Robben Island, 6 miles/10 kilometers from Cape Town, where he had to do hard labor and was allowed only one visitor every six months. When Mandela was finally freed, in 1990, he made his first public speech on the balcony of Cape Town's city hall, calling for peace and an end to apartheid.

CAPE TOWN

Located along the shore of Table Bay, on the coast of the Atlantic Ocean

SPES BONA

(Latin for "Good Hope")

The first Europeans to view the Cape were the Portuguese. Bartolomeu Dias rounded the Cape in 1488, before moving on in search of trade with the east coast of Africa. The next recorded European sighting of the Cape was by Vasco da Gama in 1497, as he was searching for a route from Europe to India.

Between August and November, southern right whales come to the coastal waters of the Cape to mate and calve, then nurse their young—often quite close to the shore.

Southern right whales are slow swimmers, making them easy whales to watch. They can be distinguished by their long, arching mouths and double blowhole. They average around 43 feet/13 meters in length and can weigh an enormous 60 tons/54 metric tons.

BOULDERS BEACH, ON THE CAPE PENINSULA, IS HOME TO A COLONY OF AFRICA'S ONLY PENGUIN SPECIES.

POPULATION: 3.7 MILLION

A tradition in Cape Town is the firing of the Noon Gun at Lion Battery on Signal Hill.

AND BACK TO SAINT PETERSBURG IN 1991.

SAINT PETERSBURG

RUSSIA'S CULTURAL CAPITAL

The city was founded by Tsar Peter the Great on May 27, 1703. He named it after his patron saint, Peter the Apostle.

FROM SAINT PETERSBURG TO PETROGRAD IN 1914, TO LENINGRAD IN 1924,

BUILT ON THE SPOT WHERE EMPEROR ALEXANDER II WAS ASSASSINATED IN 1881

THE CHURCH OF OUR SAVIOR ON THE SPILLED BLOOD

THE CITY'S NAME HAS CHANGED MANY TIMES—

The Siege of Leningrad (September 8, 1941, to January 27, 1944) was one of the longest and most destructive sieges in history.

THE FAMOUS COMPOSER SHOSTAKOVICH WAS BORN IN SAINT PETERSBURG IN 1906

The city's main street is Nevsky Prospect. It was named for Prince Alexander Yaroslavich (1221–1263), nicknamed Nevsky, who, according to legend, led a small army to defeat an attempted invasion on the banks of Saint Petersburg's Neva River.

Here you will find a palace, a cathedral, an emporium, six eighteenth-century churches, a monument to Catherine the Great, an enormous eighteenth-century shopping mall, the Russian national library, and the Anichkov Bridge, with its four famous horse sculptures.

On October 25, 1917, a blank shot from the cruiser ship Aurora marked the start of the assault on Saint Petersburg's Winter Palace—and the beginning of the October Revolution.

SAINT PETERSBURG HAS ITS OWN FLAG —A RED BACKGROUND WITH TWO SILVER ANCHORS CROSSING EACH OTHER AND A GOLDEN SCEPTER IN THE MIDDLE.

AS THE CITY HAS BOTH RIVER AND SEA PORTS.

ONE ANCHOR REFLECTS THE RIVER AND THE OTHER THE SEA,

Saint Petersburg is home to the Hermitage. Founded by Catherine the Great in 1764, it is one of the largest art museums in the world.

The green-and-white Winter Palace, once the home of imperial Russia's royal family, now houses part of the Hermitage museum. Its main facade is 820 feet/250 meters long and 100 feet/30 meters high, and the palace contains 1,786 doors, 1,945 windows, 1,500 rooms, and 117 staircases.

In order to view every exhibit in the Hermitage for a minute, a visitor would need to spend eight years there without sleep.

The Mariinsky Theater has hosted world-famous ballet dancers such as Vaslav Nijinsky, Anna Pavlova, and Rudolf Nureyev.

Saint Petersburg's home to more than 200 museums, many of them located in historic buildings.

The coastal Aboriginal Australians from Sydney called themselves the Eora — from *ee*, meaning "yes," and *ora*, meaning "place."

At 1,014 feet/309 meters, Sydney Tower is the city's tallest structure and the second-tallest observation tower in the Southern Hemisphere.

It took 1,400 workers eight years to build Sydney Harbor Bridge.

Sydney

THE MOST POPULATED CITY IN AUSTRALIA

THE SYDNEY HARBOR BRIDGE IS THE WIDEST LONG-SPAN BRIDGE IN THE WORLD.

The concert hall is famous for its poor acoustics, which have proved a challenge for performers.

About 67,000 square feet/6,223 square meters of glass were used to make the Sydney Opera House™.

The highest point of the Sydney Opera House™, the tip of the tallest shell, reaches 221 feet/67.4 meters above Sydney Harbor.

Sydney Harbor Bridge is nicknamed the "Coat Hanger."

The Sydney Opera House™ was completed in 1973. It took 10,000 construction workers 14 years to build it, with a final total cost of 102 million Australian dollars — more than 14 times the price originally intended.

A total of 233 designs were submitted for the Opera House design competition, which was open until the end of 1956. Jørn Utzon was the winner.

The discovery of stone artifacts has revealed that the Sydney region was first settled by Aboriginal Australians more than 30,000 years ago.